HALIFAX
Pictorial Guide
including Dartmouth & Bedford

Stone House Publishing Inc.

Stone House Publishing Inc.
P.O. Box 9301, Station A
Halifax, Nova Scotia, Canada   B3K 5N5

Introduction and walking tour by: Elizabeth Pacey
Directory compiled and edited by: Carol Willcocks
Graphic Design: Arthur Carter
Typesetting: A.J. Copyrite Inc.
Sales and Marketing: Susan Helpard
General Manager: J. Daniel Sargeant

Canadian Cataloguing in Publication Data
Hines, Sherman, 1941-
   Halifax pictorial guide

ISBN 0-921128-29-0

1. Halifax (N.S.) — Description - Guide-books. 2. Halifax
(N.S.) - Description — Views. I. Title.

FC2346.18.H56 1990   917.16'22   C89-098659-2
F1039.5.H17H56 1990

Printed for Stone House Publishing Inc.
in Hong Kong.

Halifax is situated on one of the finest natural harbours in the world. Stretching nine kilometres inland from the Atlantic coast, the sheltered, deep-water harbour was the most significant physical factor in the founding of Halifax. The great harbour, or "chebooktook" as the Micmac called it, was singled out by the British Lords of Trade and Plantations as the ideal site for a military and naval stronghold.

Colonel Edward Cornwallis, a 36-year old aristocrat, was charged with the daunting task of establishing the British bastion to defend the colonies against the powerful French fortress at Louisbourg. In the summer of 1749, Cornwallis sailed up the harbour aboard the sloop *Sphinx*, followed by 13 transports of settlers.

The garrison town that grew up on the shores of the great harbour has alternately flourished and struggled through more than two centuries of change. Halifax has known the heady days of sailing ships and privateering, when rich cargoes of booty were stored and sold on the waterfront. The merchants of Halifax once dared to trade with blockaded southern ports during the American Civil War. The politicians of Halifax, like Joseph Howe and Charles Tupper, were embroiled in the great Confederation debates. Halifax survived the world's most devastating pre-atomic explosion on December 6, 1917 when the munitions ship *Mont Blanc*, carrying 4,000 tons of T.N.T., collided with the *Imo* in mid-harbour. And Haligonians have witnessed the awesome departure of convoys for the raging battles of the Atlantic during World War II.

Halifax has emerged as a many-facetted urban centre that can equally well be identified as an active seaport, a major naval base and an historic provincial capital.

The port of Halifax, where the steamships of native son Samuel Cunard once docked, still hosts several luxury liners each summer. For these ships Halifax plays the role of an exciting foreign port on a cruise to the cooler northern climes. However, the main business of the port is the year-round movement of cargoes like oil, for the refineries on the Dartmouth shore, gypsum, grain and containers. More than 16 million metric tons of cargo pass through the port each year. The container traffic is the fastest-growing part of the industry. Already Halifax serves more container shipping lines and more trade routes than any other port in Canada.

A further harbourside industry is Autoport at Eastern Passage on the Dartmouth shore. Autoport is the leading automobile distribution centre in Canada. At least 24 automobile manufacturers from Canada and around the world send approximately 115,000 vehicles through the facility.

Joining the laden cargo ships in the waters of Halifax harbour are sturdy, hard-working tugboats and compact, modern passenger ferries that resemble floating spaceships. On bright, summer Sundays, the shining waters are dotted with graceful yachts, their white sails and colourful spinnakers billowing in the breeze. The familiar sight of *Bluenose II*, an exact replica of Nova Scotia's famous racing schooner, is always stirring. And every second year, the Boston Yacht Club and Royal Nova Scotia Yacht Squadron run the celebrated international yacht race from Marblehead, Massachusetts to Halifax harbour.

Halifax is also home port to the east coast fleet of the Canadian Navy. Mainstays of the fleet are combat-ready destroyers and sleek, stealthy submarines. New state-of-the-art patrol frigates, coming on stream for the 1990's, are the pride of the navy. Named for major Canadian cities, the lead frigate bears the name *HMCS Halifax*.

The Halifax metropolitan area has the largest concentration of armed forces in Canada. Canadian Forces Base (CFB) Halifax maintains the Fleet School which trains more than 12,000 people each year, the Ship Repair Unit, the 1500-acre Ammunition Depot near Bedford and many other defence-related naval activities. Across the harbour, on the Dartmouth shore, CFB Shearwater has been linked with aviation since the early years of the century, and planes based there have spanned three nationalities. In 1918, the United States Navy, under the command of Lieutenant Richard Byrd, established a seaplane base at Shearwater; Byrd later attained world recognition as a polar explorer. In 1942, Britain's Royal Navy set up a naval air station to assemble and test replacement planes for aircraft carriers on Atlantic convoy duty. By 1948, the Royal Canadian Navy took over the air station to support their own acquisition of an aircraft carrier.

As capital of Nova Scotia and part of the largest metropolitan area in the Atlantic region, Halifax is the centre for medical, educational, commercial, financial and governmental services. For example, the city has eight hospitals and six degree-granting institutions. Halifax is also a mecca for culture and entertainment. Acclaimed professional concerts and drama are offered by Symphony Nova Scotia and Neptune Theatre. The Dalhousie Arts Centre hosts numerous star-studded productions from the realm of opera, dance, comedy and music. And art galleries of all sizes and types abound.

In recent years, the scope and animation of less formal entertainment has turned Halifax into a fun-loving phenomenon. Not only are the streets of downtown Halifax alive with shops and shoppers by day, but literally dozens of pubs and restaurants make the city's nightlife an unabashed success. Extraordinary events are the Halloween Mardi Gras when thousands of costumed merrymakers parade in the streets, and the international Buskers Festival, when Haligonians and visitors are treated to innovative street performances by talented jugglers, comedians and dancers. The colourful Town Criers competition, homespun craft markets, the Halifax Natal Day Festival, and the Mayor's old-fashioned tea parties all add to the congenial and lively atmosphere.

The patina of age adds prestige and character to Nova Scotia's capital. The Halifax Citadel, an impressive star-shaped fortress with ramparts, sallyports and a soldiers' canteen, is Canada's most-visited historic site. In the downtown, there are many fine public buildings, from the classical simplicity of St. Paul's Church, the nation's oldest Protestant church, to the Georgian grandeur of Province House, and from the Victorian elegance of City Hall to the ornate exuberance of the provincial Art Gallery. Barrington Street is one of the longest commercial historic streetscapes, while the northernmost block of Granville Street is the most decorative with its tapestry of Italianate arches, colonnettes and keystones. On the waterfront, restored warehouses of ironstone and wood are tangible evidence of the city's seafaring past, while the old brewery recalls early industrial

prowess. Historic cottages, townhouses with Scottish dormers or decorative porches, and splendid Victorian and Edwardian mansions all typify the distinctive architecture of Halifax.

The man-made city is enhanced by nature's flora, foliage and green spaces. In fact, Halifax has more trees than any city of comparable size in North America. And the major parks and gardens are remarkable.

The expansive green field of the Commons is the City's and indeed the country's, oldest park. In 1760, Governor Charles Lawrence decreed that a large acreage be set aside "for the sole use and benefit of the inhabitants". While southern portions of the original acreage were eventually taken up by public buildings, the 19th century army insisted on a clear field of fire across the north portion of the Commons, thus protecting the public open space for military manoeuvres and recreation. In 1876, P.T. Barnum's circus, the "Greatest Show on Earth", played on the Commons, and in 1897, Queen Victoria's Diamond Jubilee was celebrated with the pageantry of a military tattoo. In recent years, local enthusiasts have enjoyed team sports like baseball, soccer and cricket on the Commons.

Joggers, walkers and skiers are partial to Point Pleasant Park at the tip of the Halifax peninsula. There are more than 25 miles of paths in the wooded, seaside park. Ten thousand years ago, passing glaciers polished the slate bedrock smooth; outcroppings of the native stone can be seen on the slopes of the Quarry Pond. The wild creatures of the park include salamanders, squirrels, and seals that frolic off the point in winter. Gulls soaring above the pines are reminders of the closeness of the sea. Historic forts, remnants of old batteries and the imposing Prince of Wales Tower, are reminders of the park's military era. Built in 1796, the Prince of Wales Tower was the first martello tower in the British Empire.

Near the shores of the Bedford Basin, the Hemlock Ravine Park is a significant ecological site with a rare, virgin stand of 250 to 350-year-old 80-foot high hemlocks. It was in this romantic, rural setting that Prince Edward, son of King George III and commander of the garrison, created an 18th century estate for his beautiful French mistress, known as Julie. The heart-shaped Julie's Pond still exists in the park, and one of the buildings, the classical Prince's Lodge Rotunda, stands nearby at the water's edge.

The Sir Sandford Fleming Park, along the Northwest Arm, also began as the rural retreat of a distinguished historical figure. Fleming engineered the construction of the Canadian Pacific Railway, designed the first Canadian postage stamp, which depicted the beaver, and invented the present system of time zones. He donated his estate, The Dingle, to Halifax in commemoration of the 150th anniversary of the founding of representative government. The park, with its stately memorial tower and sheltered beach, is an ideal site for watching a myriad of yachts sail past.

In the heart of Halifax on Spring Garden Road, is North America's finest example of a formal garden, the Public Gardens. To enter the gates is to enter "a dream of beauty". There are exotic trees like magnolias, a Japanese umbrella pine, and the maiden hair or ginkgo tree; there are rose bowers, floating flower beds with daffodils and hyacinths, and the colourful carpet bed where low plants form a picture. Swans glide on Griffins's Pond, and statues of mythical goddesses watch over the beauties of nature. The intricately decorated Victorian bandstand is the charming centrepiece of the Gardens.

The *Halifax Pictorial Guide* is an inviting preview of the varied and delightful amenities that await the visitor. A walking tour follows the footprints of Joseph Howe and recreates his involvement in the triumphs of history. Intimate inside views of shops and restaurants combine with scenic photographs by Sherman Hines. A native Nova Scotian, Sherman Hines graduated with highest honours from the Brooks Institute in California and has since been named Maritime and Canadian Photographer of the Year and a Fellow of the prestigious American Society of Photographers. The colourful imagery of the *Halifax Pictorial Guide* is a celebration and a lasting souvenir of Halifax and its environs.

Elizabeth Pacey is author of six books including "Georgian Halifax" and "Historic Halifax", and she has received two national awards, one from Heritage Canada and one from Environment Canada.

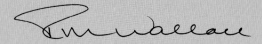

Every weekday in July and August, visitors are invited to "Tea with the Mayor". The Grand Parade provides a picture-perfect setting for the tea. In our century-old Halifax Hall, history and hospitality await you.

Ron Wallace,
Mayor, City of Halifax

The numbers which appear beside each advertiser's name in directories correspond with page numbers in pictorial section.

The numbers which appear beside each advertiser's name in directories correspond with page numbers in pictorial section.

Starting Point: Grand Parade
Duration: approximately 90 minutes

"What a book I could write if I were to go about sketching its queer old streets and snug interiors in the spirit of Dickens", said Joseph Howe of downtown Halifax. If he could return today, he would find much has changed, but many things have remained the same. The muddy streets are paved with asphalt, the wooden sidewalks have been replaced by concrete, but he could still find many of the sites and buildings he knew well.

The **Grand Parade** was familiar ground to Joseph Howe. Just a block away, where Scotia Square now stands, he attended Mr. Bromley's Royal Acadian School in the summer months of 1815 and 1816 for his only formal education. Young Howe, used to a more carefree existence at home on the shores of the North West Arm, was not a model student; he was often truant, and one former female classmate recalled that he "chased me to death on the way home". But if Howe was a wayward student, he was a good worker. He helped his father, who was Postmaster, in the small post office across from the Grand Parade where the Bank of Commerce is now located. Years later, one of Howe's greatest victories was celebrated on the Grand Parade. Although Nova Scotia had joined Confederation, an overwhelming majority of anti-Unionists were elected in the 1867 elections. When Howe, leader of the anti-Unionists, returned to Halifax from his constituency in Hants County, he was conveyed by a splendid carriage and six horses in a torch-light procession to the Grand Parade, where he made a victory speech.

Before leaving the Parade, glance up George Street to the **Old Town Clock**. Howe immortalized his admiration for this unique building which set "a good example to all the idle chaps about the town" in a poem:

Thou grave old Time Piece, many a time and oft
I've been your debtor for the time of day;
And every time I cast my eyes aloft,
And swell the debt — I think 'tis time to pay.
Thou, like a sentinel upon a tower,
Hast still announced "the enemy's" retreat,
And now that I have got a leisure hour,
Thy praise, thou old Repeater, I'll repeat.

Proceed along Barrington St. past **St. Paul's Church**. On February 2, 1828, Joseph Howe and Susan Ann McNab of McNab's Island were married quietly by Archdeacon Willis of St. Paul's. Neither Howe nor his bride were Anglican, but the dissenting churches were not authorized to perform marriages by licence at that time. One of their ten children, John, was baptized in St. Paul's on August 17, 1848.

Turn left down Prince St. and left again onto Granville St. Howe spent many of his most exciting days as a newspaper editor and publisher in the area around **Province House**. After his apprenticeship in the printing trade, Howe, at the age of 22, published *The Acadian and General Advertiser* with his friend James Spike. In 1828, Howe purchased *The Novascotian* for £1,050 from George Renny Young. By 1829, he had formed a one-man press gallery in the House of Assembly. He began publishing a series of "Legislative Reviews" which annoyed some members who felt that there was no need to inform the people about government business. In the 1840's he lived and worked in a house where 1724 Granville St. now stands.

Turn right at George St. and walk down to the water's edge just past Fisherman's Market, which housed British Army Commissary Stores in Howe's day. Here, at the **Market Slip**, Howe would often go for a late-night swim after working long hours at his printing shop. It was probably from here, too, that the energetic young Howe rowed across to McNab's Island to court Susan Ann. Though Capt. McNab, Susan Ann's father, first expressed "horror and indignation" at this courtship, Howe's persistence won out.

As you walk back up the south side of George St. you will pass the site of the first office where Howe published *The Novascotian*, at the corner of Bedford Row and George Street.

Across Bedford Row, where the **Old Post Office** (now Art Gallery) stands, a large wooden structure once housed the office where Howe worked as an apprentice printer for his father, John Howe, who published *The Gazette*. Years later, Howe would have witnessed the construction of this fine sandstone building with interest. The building typified the federal-provincial struggle in which Howe played a leading role at the time of Confederation. Nova Scotia began constructing this post office and customs building prior to Confederation. After Confederation, the federal government claimed the building because postal and customs services had become federal responsibilities. The controversy was finally settled when the federal government agreed to pay half the cost of construction.

Cross Hollis St. and enter the grounds of **Province House**. This building was the setting for Howe's greatest triumphs. In 1835, Howe's famous libel trial was held in the court room (now Legislative Library) of Province House. Howe spoke for six and a quarter hours in his own defense, arguing for freedom of the press. After his acquittal, a cheering crowd carried him home. Howe was first elected to the House of Assembly in 1836; he began strongly,

advocating responsible government, religious equality and more control of revenues by the House of Assembly. Once, when Howe became incensed at the private meetings of the 12 powerful appointed members of the Legislative Council, he banged a hole in the wall of the Red Room with his cane. Eventually Howe himself became Premier in 1860 and held the post until his party was defeated in 1863.

At the south end of Province House, you will see **Joe Howe's statue**. The 27½ foot monument was unveiled in 1904. The statue's pose was modelled on a description of the living Howe given by a colleague, Laurence O'Connor Doyle, in the House of Assembly. "See him with his coat thrown back, his arm upraised, his finger pointed, the angry spot on his brow; no stammer then, no lack of imagery or of ideas, but one continued stream like molten lead upon the heads of his opponents, while they stand withering, writhing beneath the purgatorial fire..." At the base of the statue, two bas relief sculptures depict scenes from Howe's life. On the south side is the scene of Howe's libel trial and on the north side, Howe is addressing the House of Assembly on his plan for an intercolonial railway system to link Halifax to Maine and Quebec. He dreamed of the day when people could "make the journey from Halifax to the Pacific in five or six days". In 1854, Howe was appointed Chief Commissioner of the Railway Board, and ten months later, the first section of the line was open for traffic.

After leaving the grounds of Province House, continue along Hollis St. to the corner of Prince St. The **eight pre-Confederation buildings** (Founders Square) on the southeast corner became the centre of the thriving press in Howe's day. The heated controversy over Confederation was debated in the newspapers published in these buildings. At **5144 Prince St.**, the third building down from the corner, William Annand published Howe's old newspaper, *The Novascotian*, as well as *The Morning Chronicle*. Jonathan McCully, later a father of Confederation, had become editor in 1857. So strongly did he support Confederation, that Annand fired him in 1865 and Howe again took over the editorship. Howe wrote a famous series of editorials opposing Confederation or the "Botheration Scheme" as he termed it. McCully purchased *The Journal* which was published in the **Steam Press Building**, around the corner at 1691 Hollis St. He renamed the newspaper *The Unionist*

and Journal and continued to support Confederation in its pages. The debate was an emotional one; both Howe and McCully engaged in sarcastic jibes and verbal mud-slinging. *The Reporter*, also published in the Steam Press Building, advocated Confederation. Next door, in the long brick **Victoria Building**, however, Messrs. McDonald and Garvie published *The Citizen*, which attacked Confederation.

Howe's lawyer, Peter Lynch, had his office in the Victoria Building. One can imagine that Howe, who got into so many scrapes, often sought legal advice.

The mansion at **1459 Hollis** was originally built about 1863 for the Hon. Benjamin Wier, who was on the Executive Council or Provincial Cabinet with Howe for many years. The house was later occupied by Sir Adams G. Archibald, a father of Confederation and one of Howe's strongest opponents.

Now look across at **Government House**. In Howe's day, the main entrance was on Hollis St. During the fight for responsible government, Lieutenant-Governor Sir Colin Campbell resisted change and Howe instigated his removal from office. His successor, Lord Falkland, proved no better and became Howe's bitter enemy. Falkland insinuated in a dispatch to the Colonial Office that the reformers were "reckless and insolvent men". Howe replied angrily that some colonists might "horsewhip a Lieutenant-Governor". Ironically, years later in 1873, Howe himself was chosen Lieutenant-Governor.

Across the street from the Victoria Building you will pass the **Halifax Club**, built in 1862. The original members of this exclusive gentlemen's club included many of Howe's political allies, such as Sir William Young and the Hon. Benjamin Wier, and his arch opponents, the Hon. J.W. Johnston and Sir Charles Tupper. Not surprisingly, Howe himself, a man-of-the-people, was not a charter member. Proceed south for two blocks. In the 19th Century, many citizens lived in what we now know as the downtown area. Howe and his associates were no exception. When you reach Salter St., cross to the east or downhill side of Hollis. You will have a good view of the granite **Black-Binney House** on the opposite side. For a number of years this was the residence of James Boyle Uniacke, who was, at first, Howe's adversary and, later, a long-term and close ally during the fight for responsible government in Nova Scotia. In 1848, after years of struggle, James Boyle Uniacke became Premier in the first truly responsible government. Howe became Provincial Secretary.

Government House was Howe's last home. He died here in the early morning hours of June 1, 1873, just three weeks after he was appointed Lieutenant-Governor. While his body lay in state in the north wing, great crowds gathered to pay their respects. *The Novascotian* summed up Howe's career. "No British North American approached him in breadth of statesman-like view — no one was his literary equal — no one could compare with him in favourably impressing a popular assembly. From 1827 until the day of his untimely death 'Joe Howe' has been the head and front to all great political changes in Nova Scotia."

In the next block, the Georgian stone house at **1335 Hollis** was built about 1835 for Sir Rupert George. He had been appointed Provincial Secretary in 1813 at the age of 17 and held the post until 1848. In 1840, when Howe criticized the extravagance of the Provincial Secretary's office as being "not worth the money", Rupert George challenged Howe to a duel. At that time, Rupert George had a reputation of being a crack shot. Howe, who felt the matter was trivial, replied that he "could not think of making a target of himself for everyone to shoot at who imagined he had a grievance". In 1848, when Howe became the first elected representative to be named to the post of Provincial Secretary, Sir Rupert George at first refused to give up the position. He was finally persuaded to do so, and the first responsible government began to function.

When you reach the corner of Morris St., glance down at the row of Georgian-style townhouses. In the 1860's, the fourth house from the corner, **5137 Morris**, was the home of William Annand, one of Howe's closest allies. Annand became Premier of the province in 1867 while still a resident of this house. Both Annand and Howe fought

against Confederation, and only when Howe refused to support the movement for the repeal of the BNA Act did Annand criticize Howe.

Turn right up Morris St. The large double house at **5184 Morris** was once the home of John Halliburton and his father, Sir Brenton Halliburton, Chief Justice and member of the ruling Council of Twelve. During the fight for responsible government, in 1840, John Halliburton claimed that Howe had insulted his father. He challenged Howe to a duel which took place in Point Pleasant Park. Halliburton fired and missed. Howe fired into the air saying, "I will not deprive an aged father of an only son."

In 1848, Howe himself lived further up Morris St. in a stone house, since replaced.

Turn right at Barrington St. and walk along the east or downhill side. You will pass **1333 Barrington**, one of the oldest Georgian houses in the city, dating back to 1817. Originally, the house was the residence of Thomas N. Jeffrey, another member of the powerful Council of Twelve and Collector of Imperial Customs, easily the most lucrative position in the Maritimes.

The **stone house** of 1828 at the corner of Barrington and Bishop Streets was the home of the Rev. George Munro Grant, minister of St. Matthew's Church and Joe Howe's first biographer.

Pause in front of Government House. You will have a good view across the street to the **Sebastopol Monument**, erected about 1860 to commemorate the Crimean War. In 1855, Joe Howe went to the United States on a recruiting campaign, as British forces in the Crimea needed reinforcement. While he was away, a small anti-British faction in Halifax alleged, in a New York newspaper, that Howe's activities were illegal. A warrant was issued for Howe's arrest. He escaped back to Nova Scotia but his secretary was caught and imprisoned. "There is no prison so loathsome in which I would not cheerfully have spent five years, to have placed five regiments under the walls of Sebastopol," said Howe.

From where you stand, you can also see **St. Matthew's Church**, next to Government House. Howe attended St. Matthew's with his wife Susan Ann, a Presbyterian. Howe himself had been brought up in the Sandemanian tradition, which advocated a return to the simple faith and teachings of Christ.

Turn up Spring Garden Road. On your right is **St. Mary's Basilica** which changed both its name and its appearance during Howe's lifetime. Prior to 1833, the church was known as St. Peter's, and during the 1860's and early 1870's, the interior and exterior were transformed into the present ornate Gothic style. As a member and one-time President of the Charitable Irish Society, Joe Howe attended services here on St. Patrick's Day.

On the opposite side of the street is the **Old Court House**. Given Howe's proclivity for legal matters, he would have noted the construction of this solid edifice after the architectural competition in 1858. Toronto architect Cyrus Thomas submitted the winning design.

Continue up Spring Garden Road for several blocks. Cross South Park St. to the **Public Gardens**. In 1833 and 1836, Joe Howe wrote editorials in *The Novascotian* advocating the formation of an Horticultural Society. He believed that such a society would "soften the acerbity of political contention" among men who could meet" in a "spirit of kindness and moderation". Though Howe was admittedly not a gardener, he thought there was no place "more abounding in gentle thoughts, and kindly inspiration, than the garden". Howe also believed that while gardens "embellish and chasten the lives of the rich" they should not be "denied to the poor". Accordingly, the Horticultural Society was organized with Joe Howe on the managing committee, and The Public Garden was soon opened.

Halifax, with its seaside setting, parks and gardens, has been a great inspiration to me as a professional photographer. The city's historic architecture has provided me with a treasure chest of visual discoveries. Seeking to capture the dramatic variety and breadth of Halifax is always new and rewarding.

For example, the Old Town Clock is an often-photographed landmark, but a close-up of the domed belfry at sunrise yielded a fresh photographic experience. For me, dusk is a favorite time of day to take interesting photographs. Here I have shown technological subjects like the bridge and the crane against the soft mauve sky of the early evening. In the Public Gardens, it is easy to find a beautiful and unique view with flowers in the foreground.

The other scenic photographs of my personal tour are found throughout the *Halifax Pictorial Guide*. The photos are indexed on pages 142 and 143; I have included comments and a few practical tips for those who want to follow the tour. Don't forget to take along enough film and your own imagination!

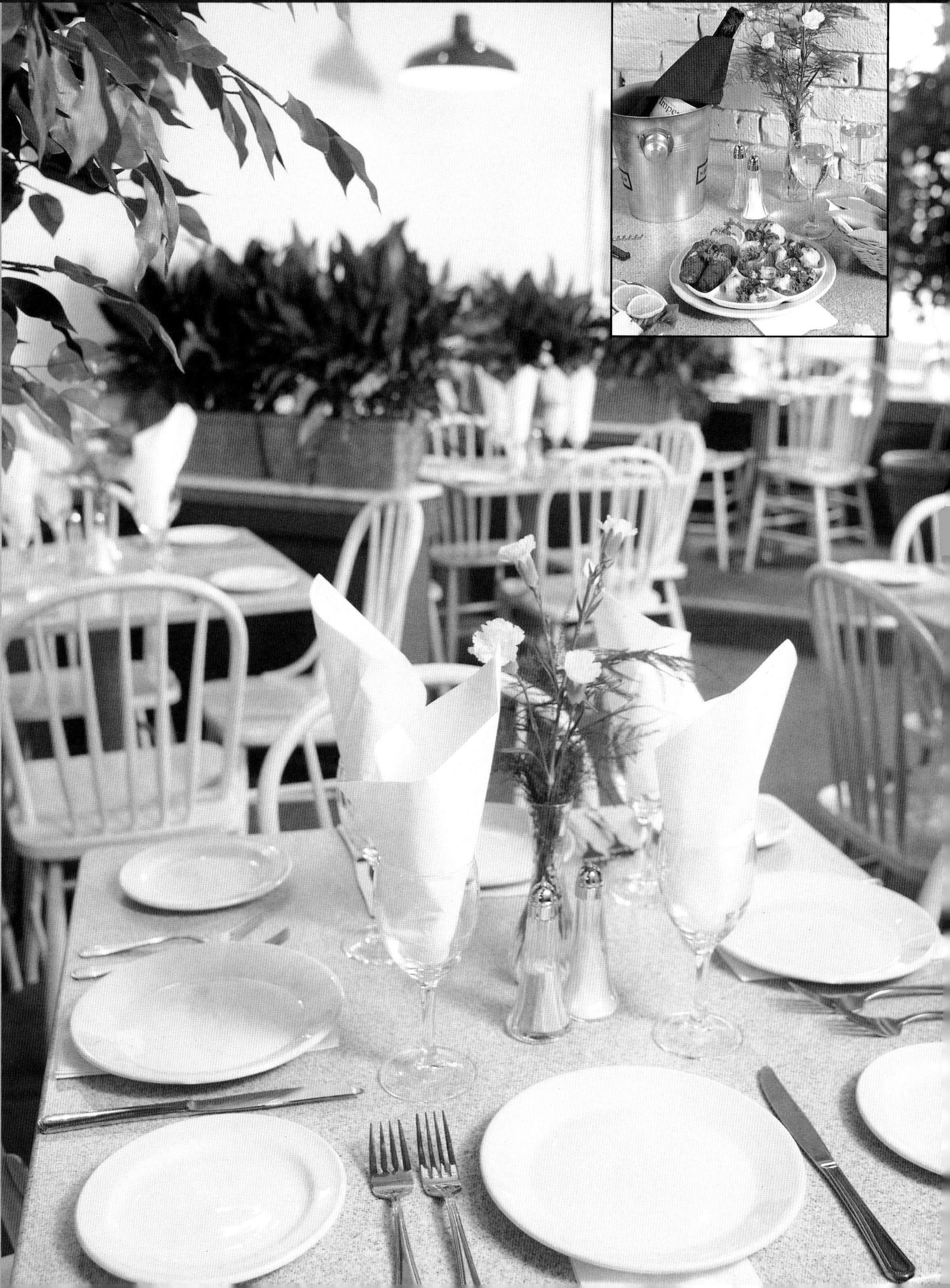

The Five Fishermen Restaurant
1740 Argyle Street

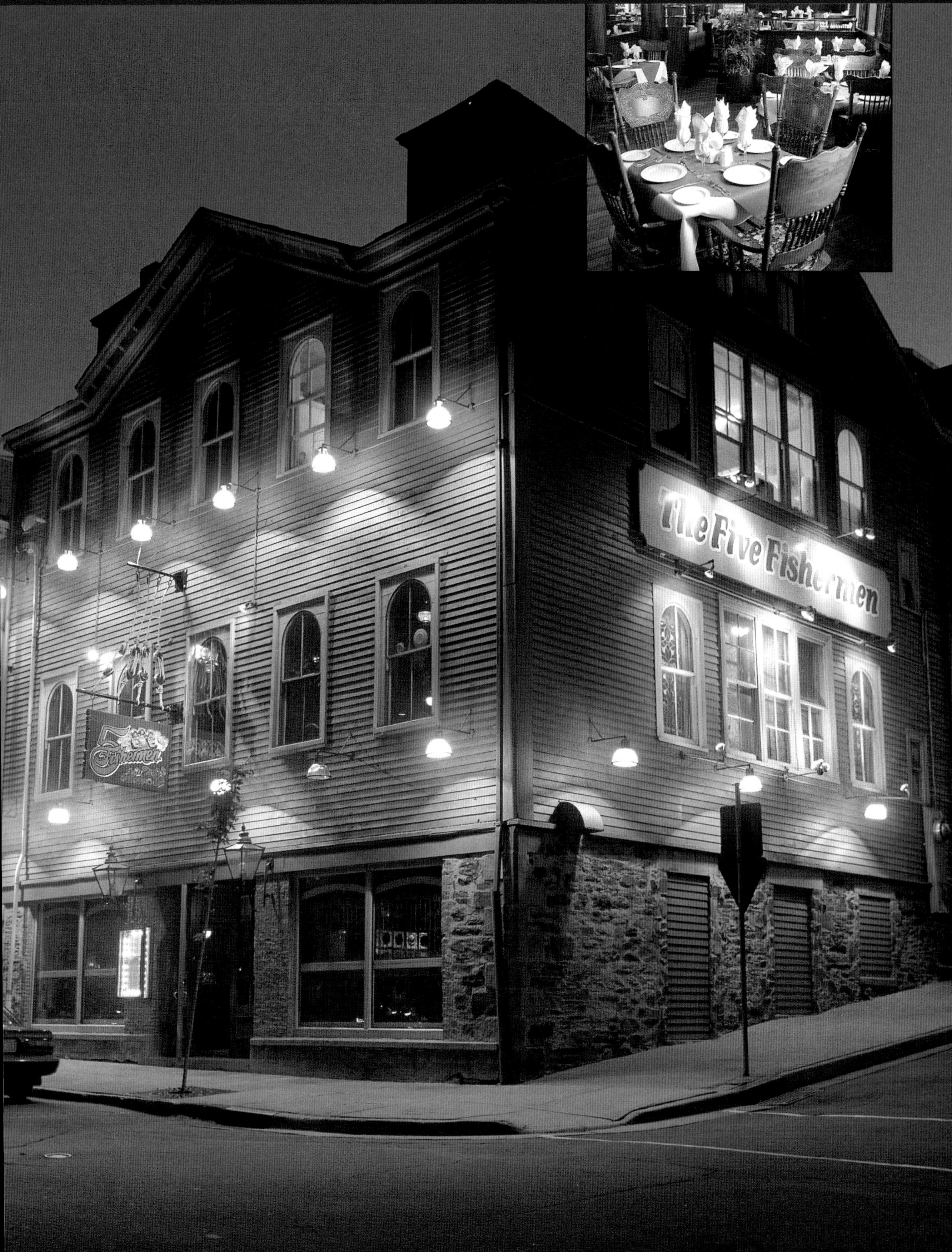

Classic Shoes

Lady Janes Accessories

Daskalides' Authentic Belgian Chocolates

BARRINGTON PLACE

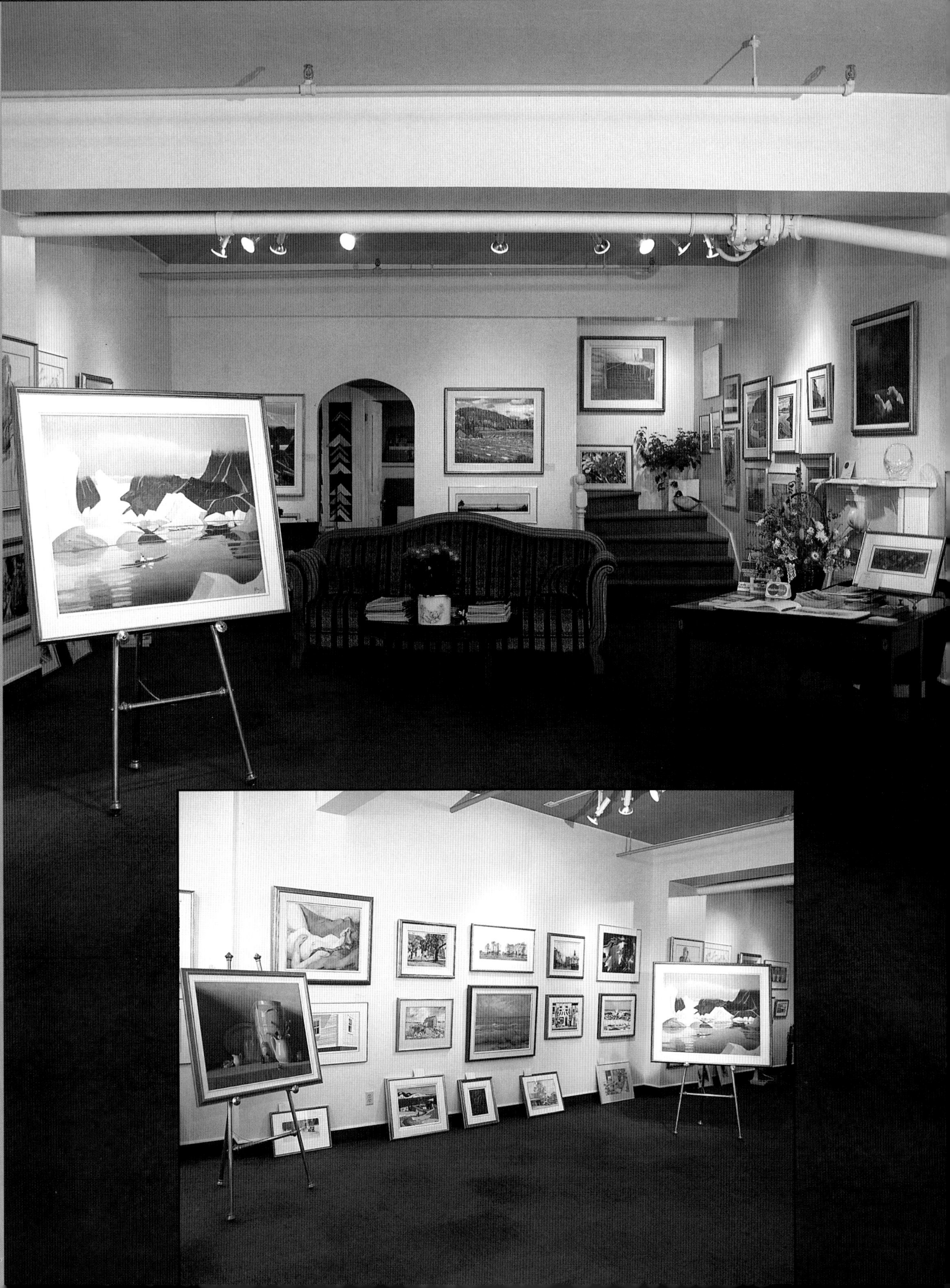

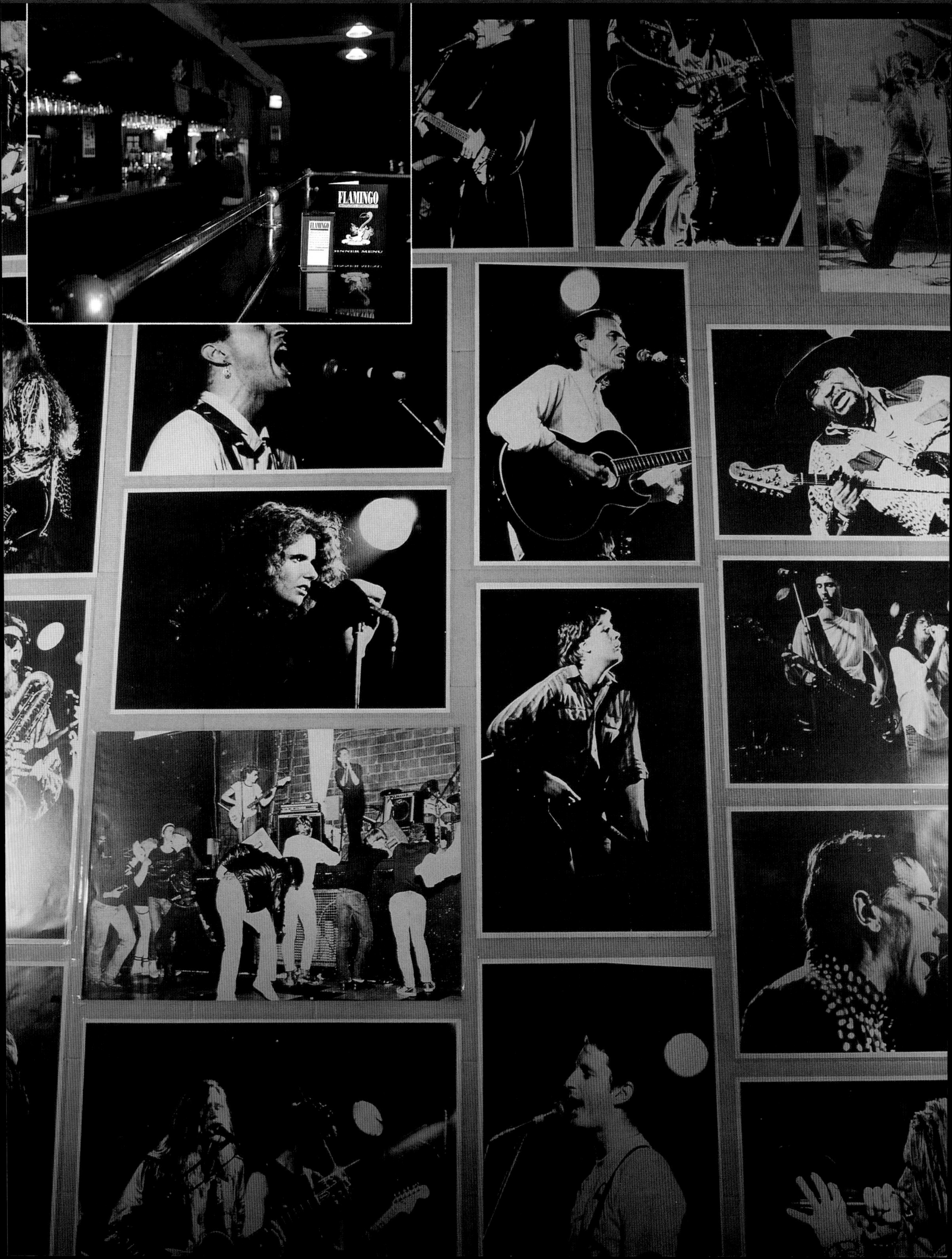
FLAMINGO
FLAMINGO
DINNER MENU

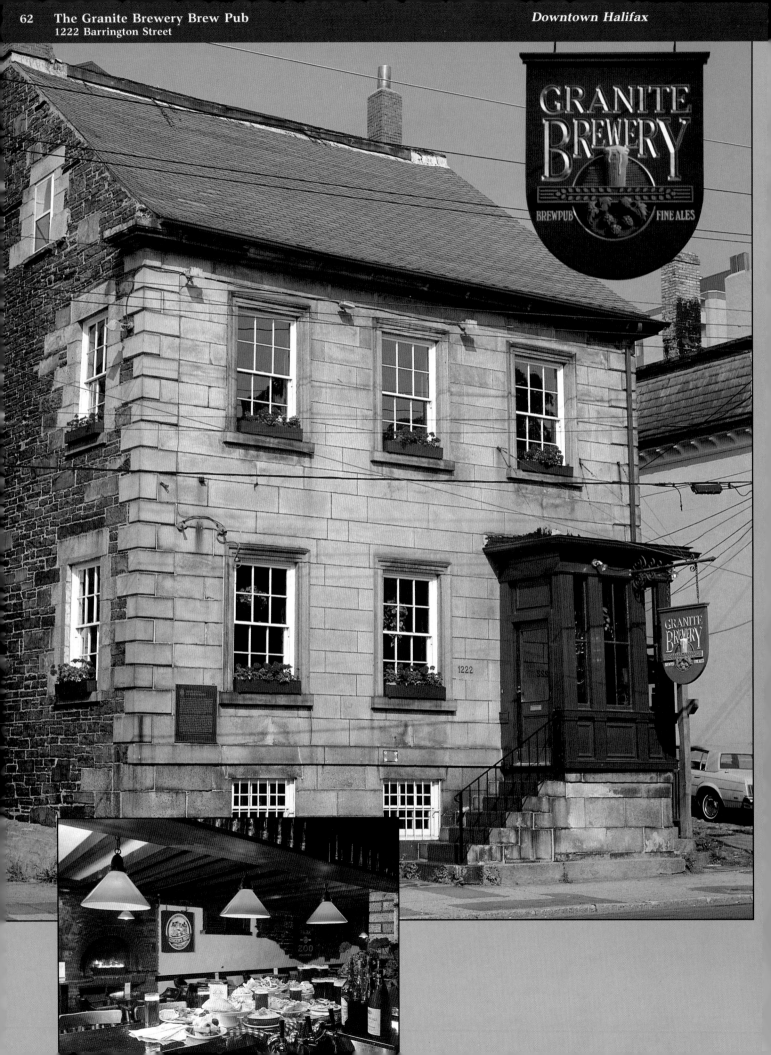

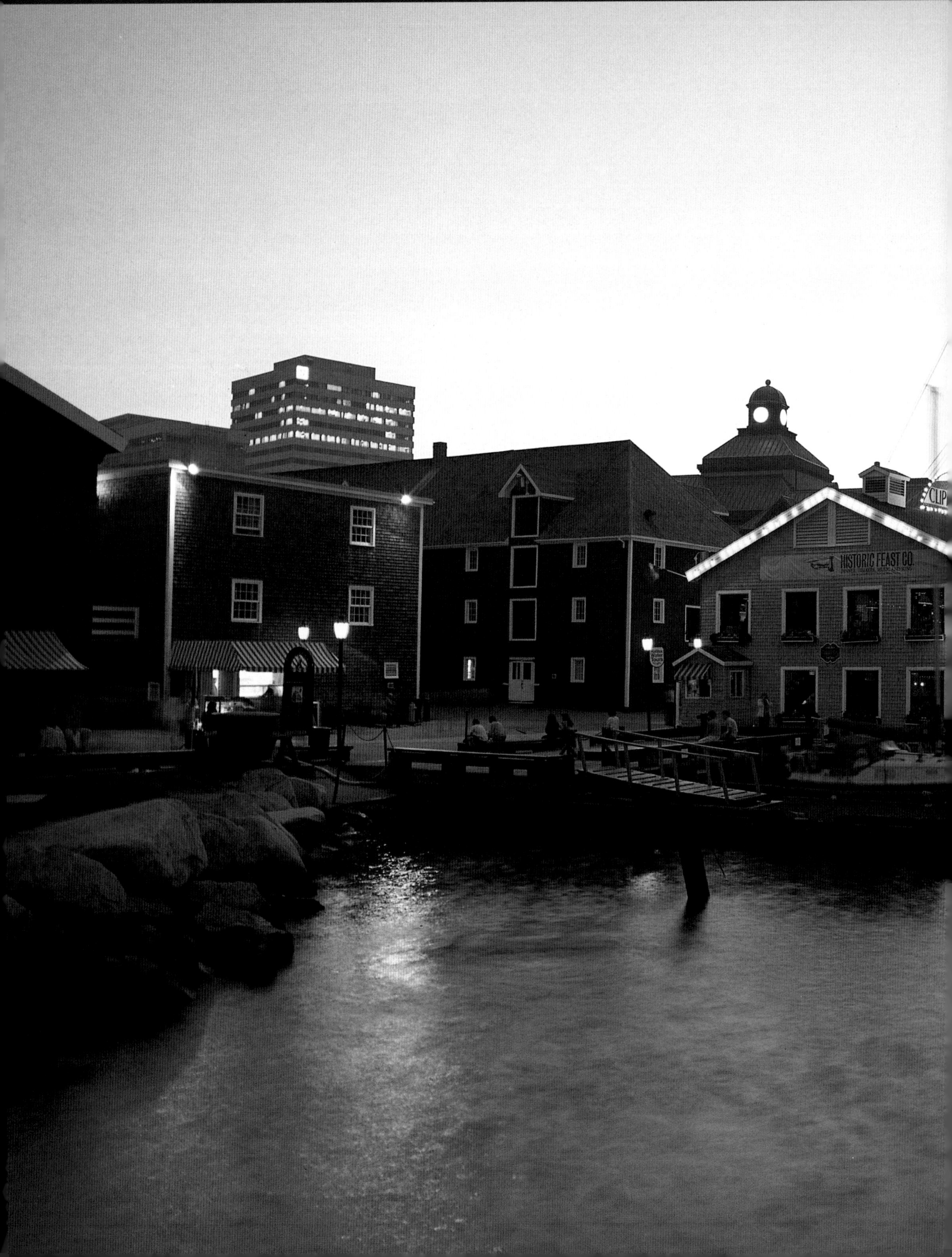
HISTORIC FEAST CO.

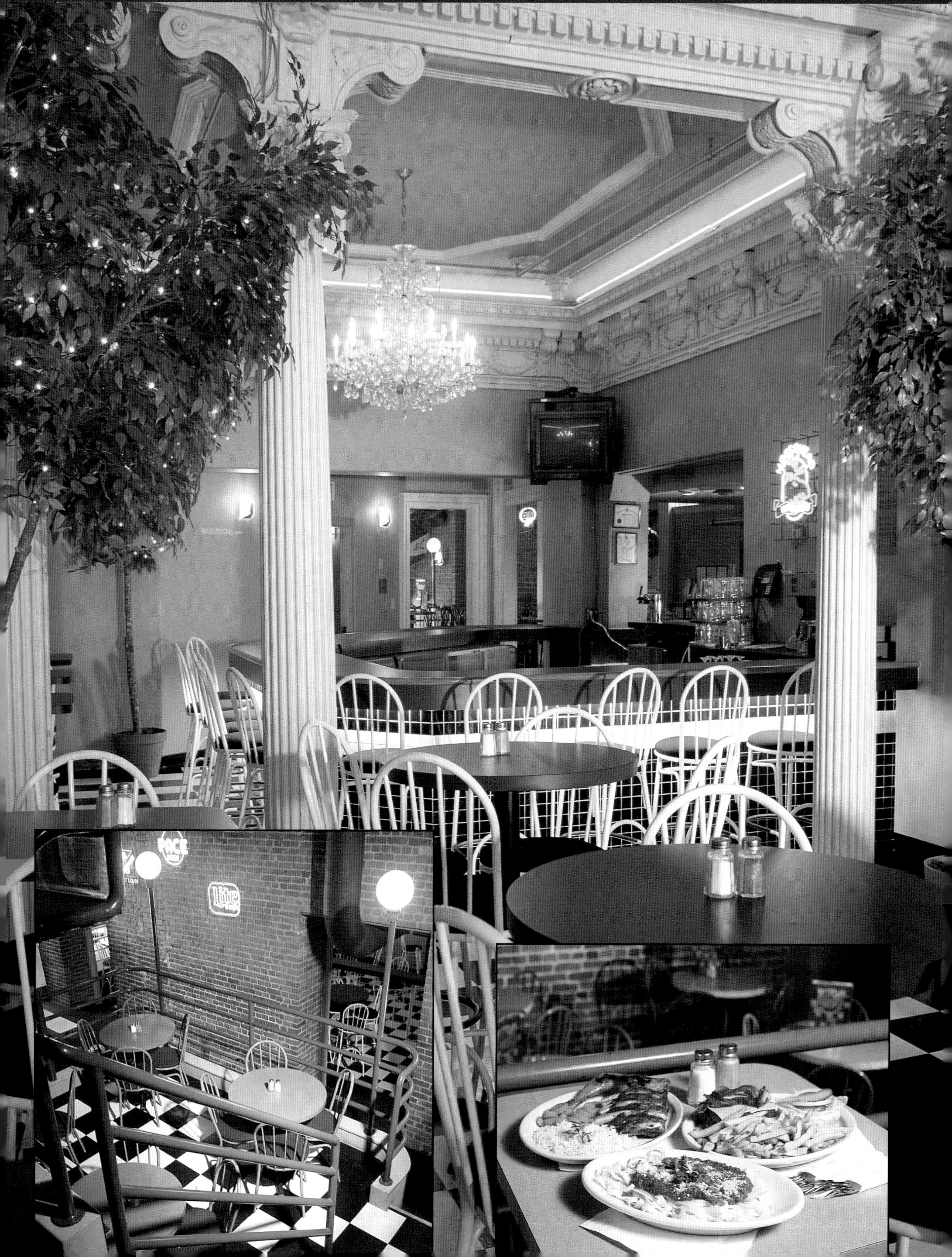
PACE
Lite

The Pewter House

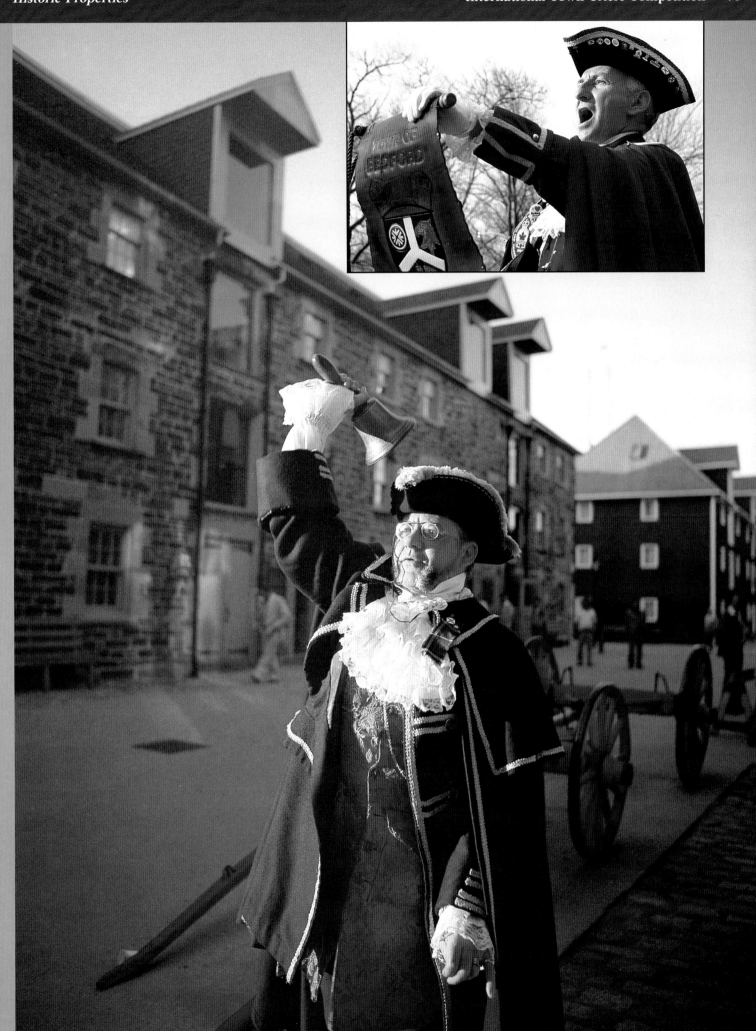

Shopping, Strolling, Dining Delight!

Moneysworth & Best

The Greenery Florists

Food Court

CLUB MONACO
QUALITY WEAR

The Club Monaco
gift certificate
IS AVAILABLE IN
ANY DENOMINATION
FOR ANY NAME
ON YOUR LIST.

The Club Monaco Gift Certificate is available in any Denomination for any Name on Your List. Always the Right Size, Style and Colour.

THE UTILITY PANT
A modern basic in 100% cotton
$49

CLUB MONACO
FRAGRANCE

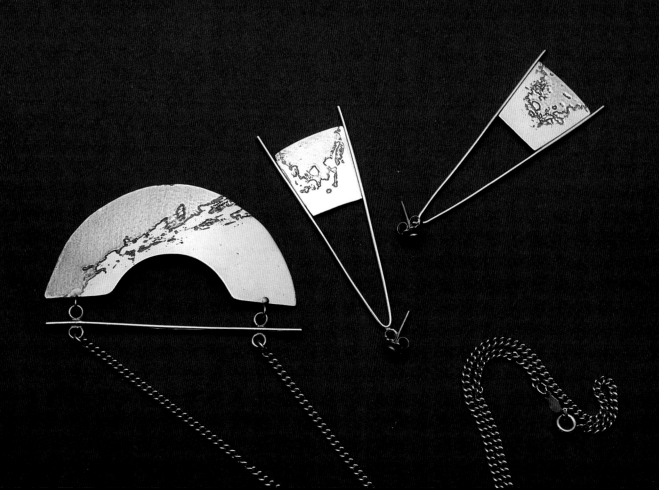

DESIGNED·TO·MATCH

JACQUES VERT

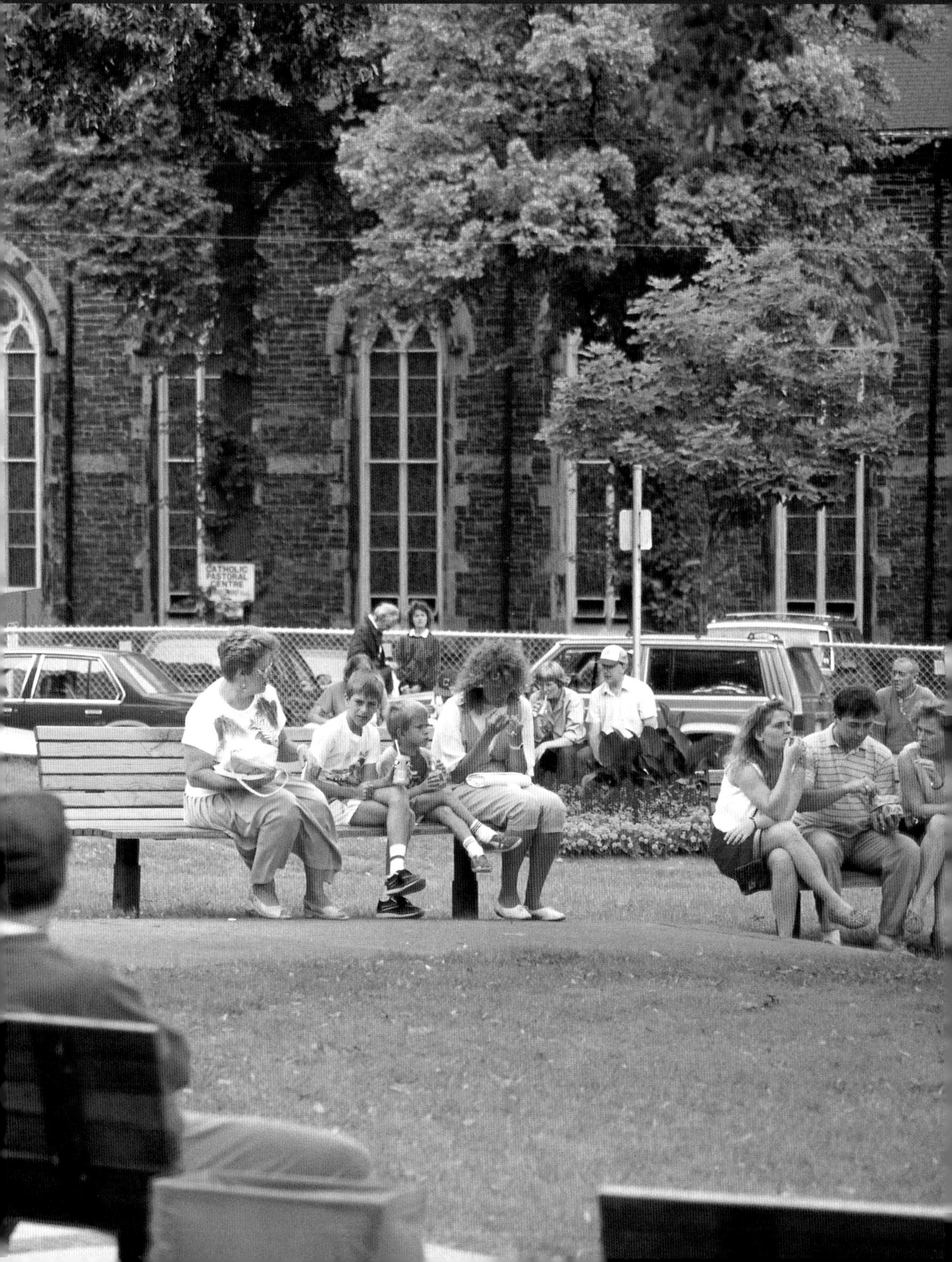
CATHOLIC
PASTORAL
CENTRE

The Wardrobe Too

Lady Deanna Shops

La Femme Lingerie

Lifestyle Fashions

Rye 'N' Pickle

Bratz Childrens Wear

The Bakery

GARDEN GOURMET COFFEE SHOP
Quality Coffee Beans — Imported Teas
Freshly Brewed Coffee

FROG HOLLOW BOOKS

Frog Hollow Books

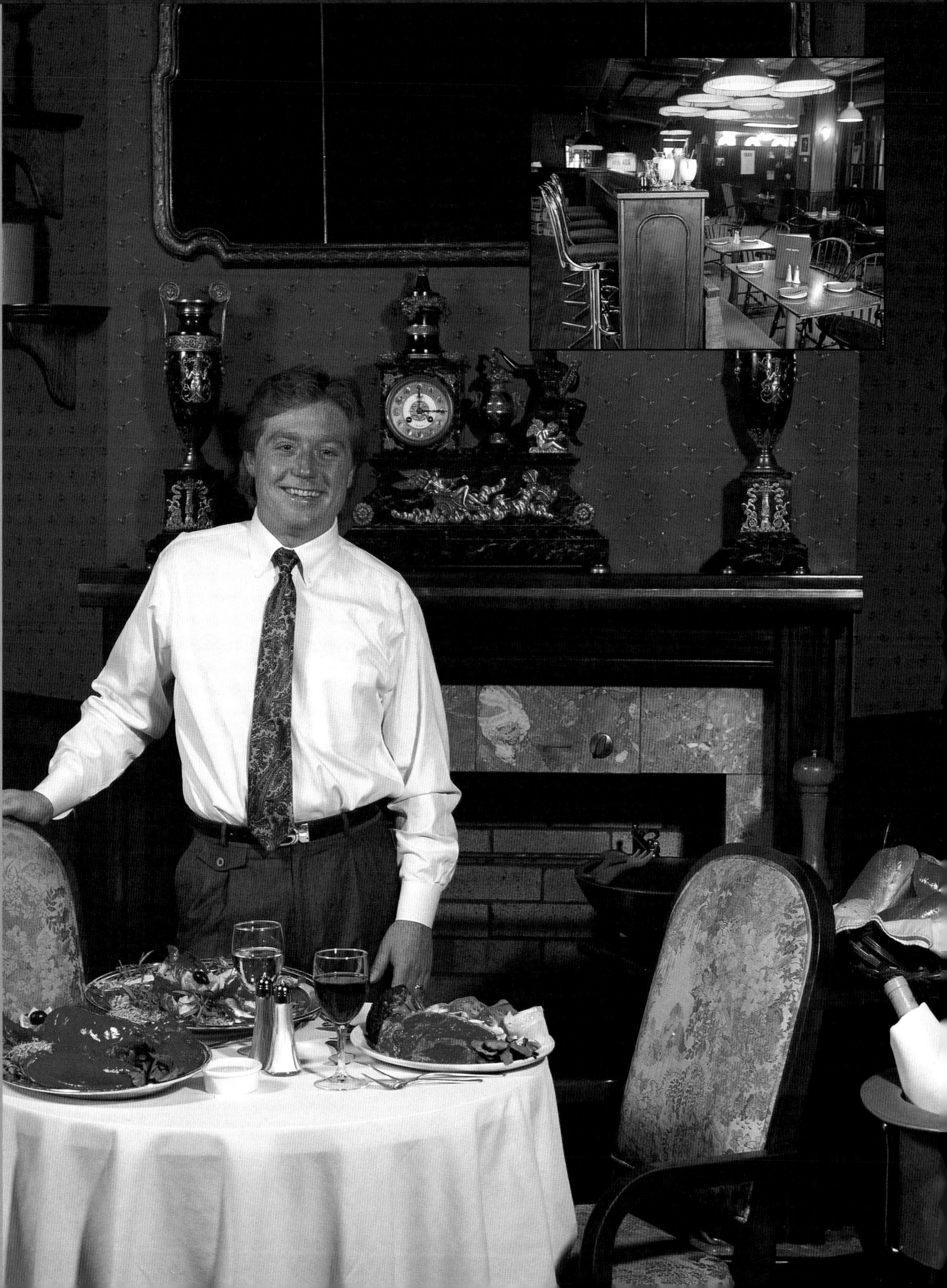

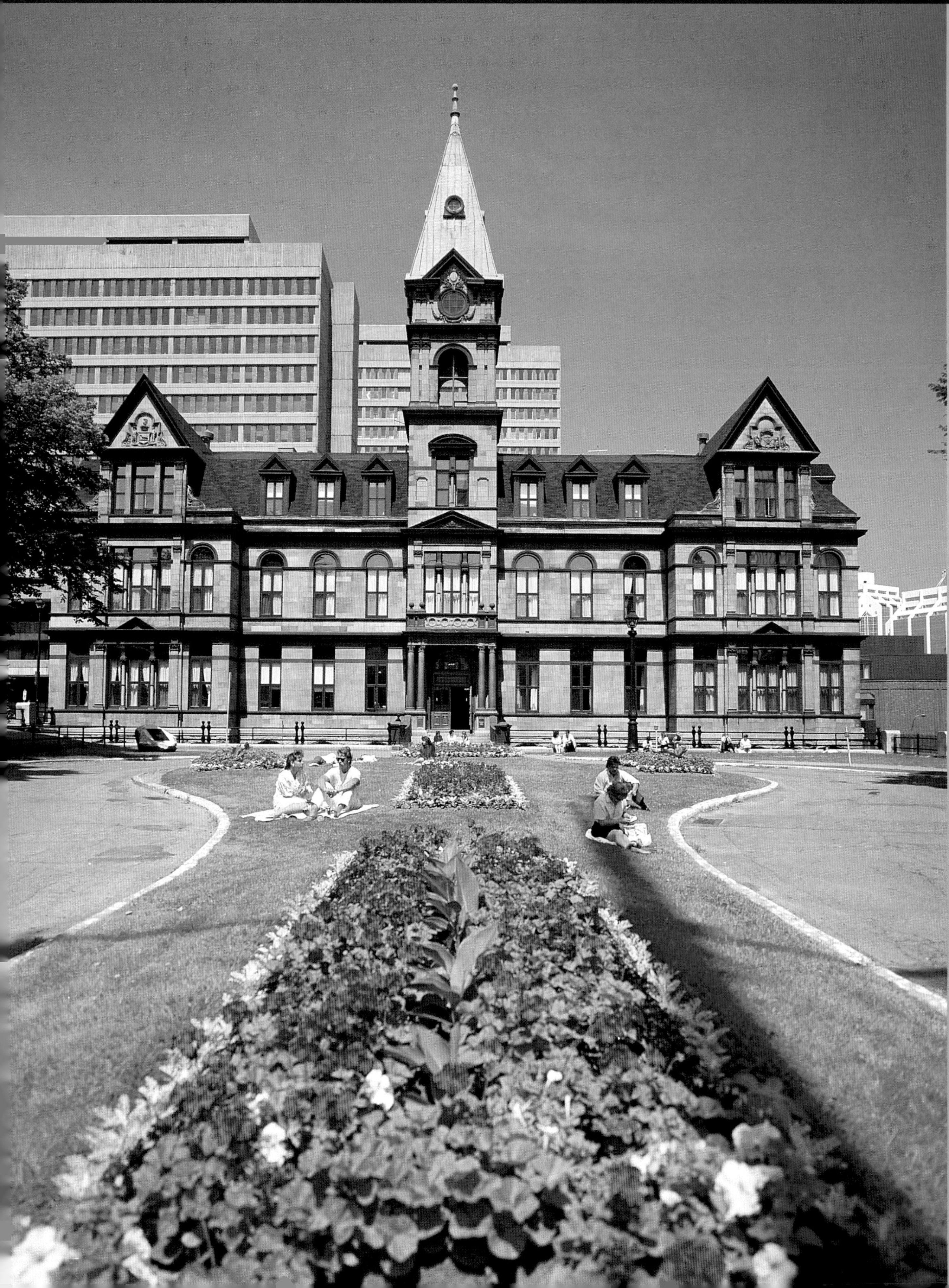

Spring Garden Road Area

Cricklewood Giftware Inc.
1529 Birmingham Street

Container Terminal
Halifax Waterfront

111

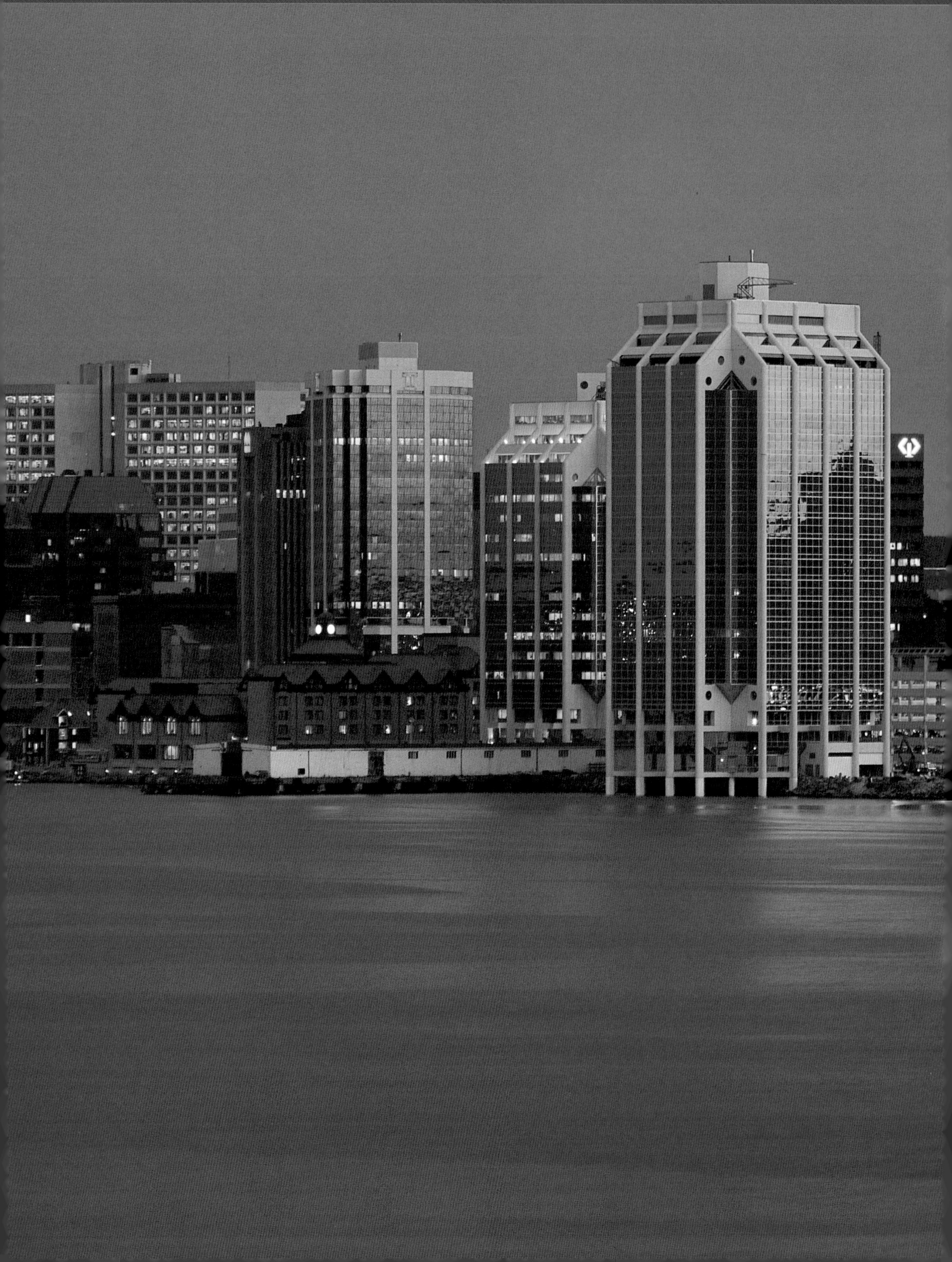

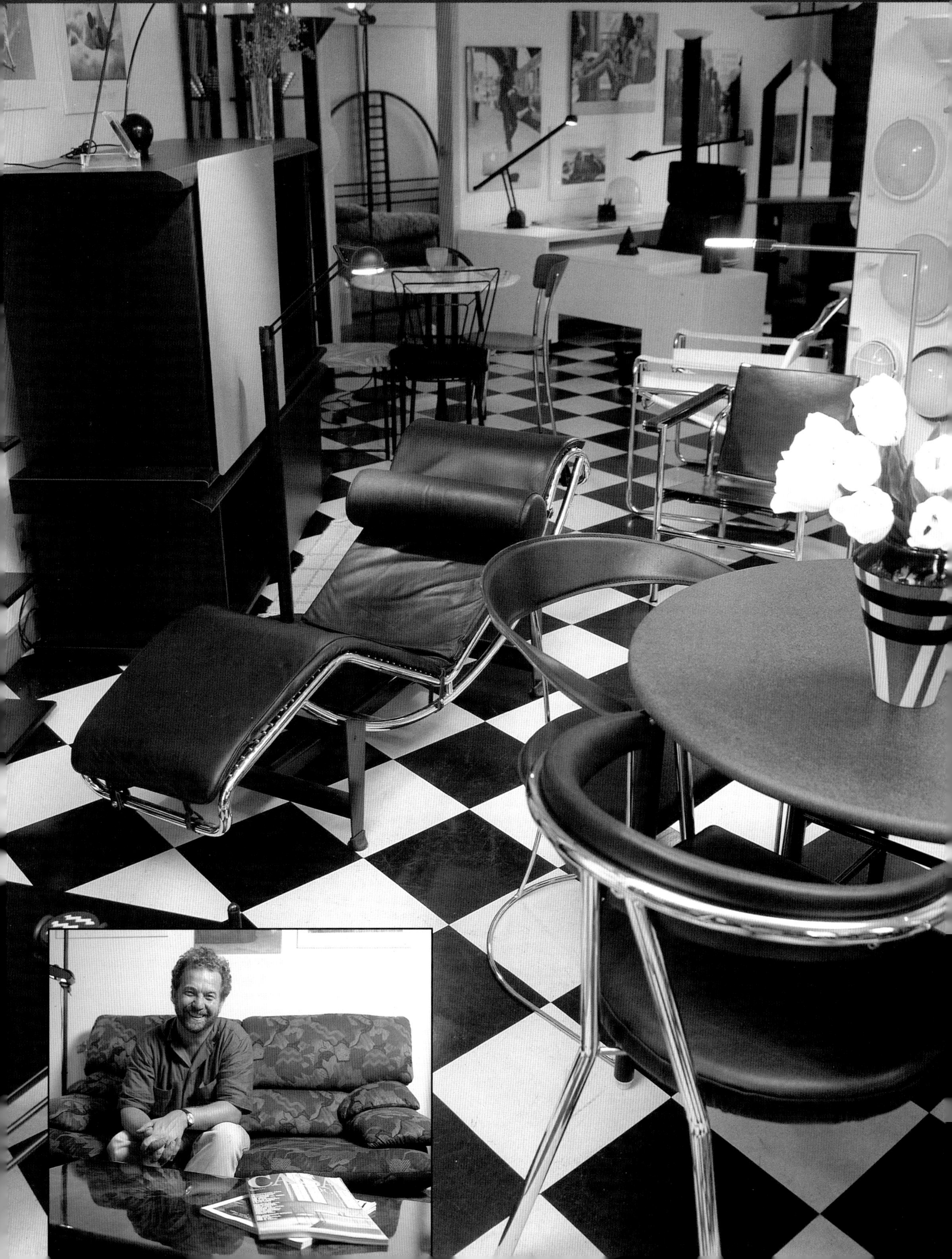
CASA

Old Town Clock (title page): Floodlit buildings work well, but be sure photos are taken before dark while there is still natural light. 1 sec. at f8, Fuji film ISO 100.

Art Gallery of Nova Scotia (page 2): Because of ongoing restoration work, I created a horizontal image, omitting one side of the building. The people in the doorway show the scale of the structure and indicate that it is open to the public.

Province·House (page 12). The late afternoon sunlight bathes the stone building with warm light and brings out the texture and roundness of the details. 100 ISO film, 35 mm Contax camera with 210 mm zoom lens, 1/30 sec. at f16.

St. Mary's Basilica (page 17): I chose the Old Burying Ground as my vantage point for photographing the Basilica; the cemetery makes a more attractive foreground than the street. With the 18 mm wide angle lens, I was able to include the decorative wrought iron fence. Expose for highlights making sure dark areas do not influence meter reading.

Halifax Waterfront (page 65): Anyone may take a photo with the soft blue and pink tones of dusk accented with bright lights. Be sure to use a tripod and make a few extra exposures. 1 sec. at f8 or 1/2 sec. at f8, 2 sec. at f8, and 4 sec. at f8, 100 ISO film.

Bluenose II (page 74): To make photos of your vacation more interesting, try the photo-journalist's approach — one overview of the setting with related close-ups of people and details. Bluenose: 1/25 sec. at f11. Inset: 1/125 sec. between f5.6 and f8.

Old Town Clock (page 77): The magic of this image is in the combination of the evening's darkness and the light reflecting off the face of the clock. Read your meter carefully and make two additional exposures. 1 sec. at f11, also try 2 sec. at f11 and 1/2 sec. at f11.

Spring Garden Road (page 78): Taken at dusk, this time exposure records the moving lights of the traffic. Different exposures will give different results. Time exposure of 2 sec. at f8.

Spring Garden Road (pages 96-97): Photos of everyday life are especially striking when bold subjects are added. Here the statue is a focal point.

Halifax City Hall (page 104): It is most important to get the light on the front of City Hall before shadows of other buildings obscure it. The green lawns and well-saturated colours of the flowers add interest to the foreground. 28 mm lens, 1/25 sec. at f16.

Buskers Festival (page 107): The white church is the perfect background for the silhouette of the figure. The contrast can be accentuated by exposing for the background, making the foreground figures go very dark. 1/250 sec. at f16, 100 ISO Fuji film.

Public Gardens (pages 108-109): I have chosen the flowers as the main subject with the bandstand as the background. It is important to use a wide angle lens in close proximity to the flowers. Also, use your polarizer for excellent colour, and try several angles. 100 ISO Fuji film, 1/125 sec. at f11.

Halifax Skyline (pages 120-121): A telephoto lens brings the details closer from across the harbour. Choose a brightly lit area of the skyline but reduce the flare from the lights by not selecting your largest aperture. 800 mm lens, f8 or f11 with longer exposure time recommended, 100 ISO film.

Macdonald Bridge (page 130): I don't often rely on sunset alone as the subject of a photo. In this case, sunset enhances the background and foreground. Try both underexposed and overexposed shots. Meter f5.6 at 1/15 sec., also at f5.6 try 1/30, 1/60, 1/125, 1/10, 1/5, 1/4, 1/2. 100 ISO Fuji film.

The Dingle at Sunset (page 134): A telephoto lens was used to compress subject matter. Be sure to bracket exposures over and under. 210 mm lens, 1/60 at f8, 100 ISO film.

Historic Architecture (pages 138-139): This variety of architectural photos shows the wealth of material just waiting to be photographed! In some cases, a detail makes a fine composition, while in others, an entire building is best. For architectural photos, it is necessary to have good lighting to give shape, form and texture.

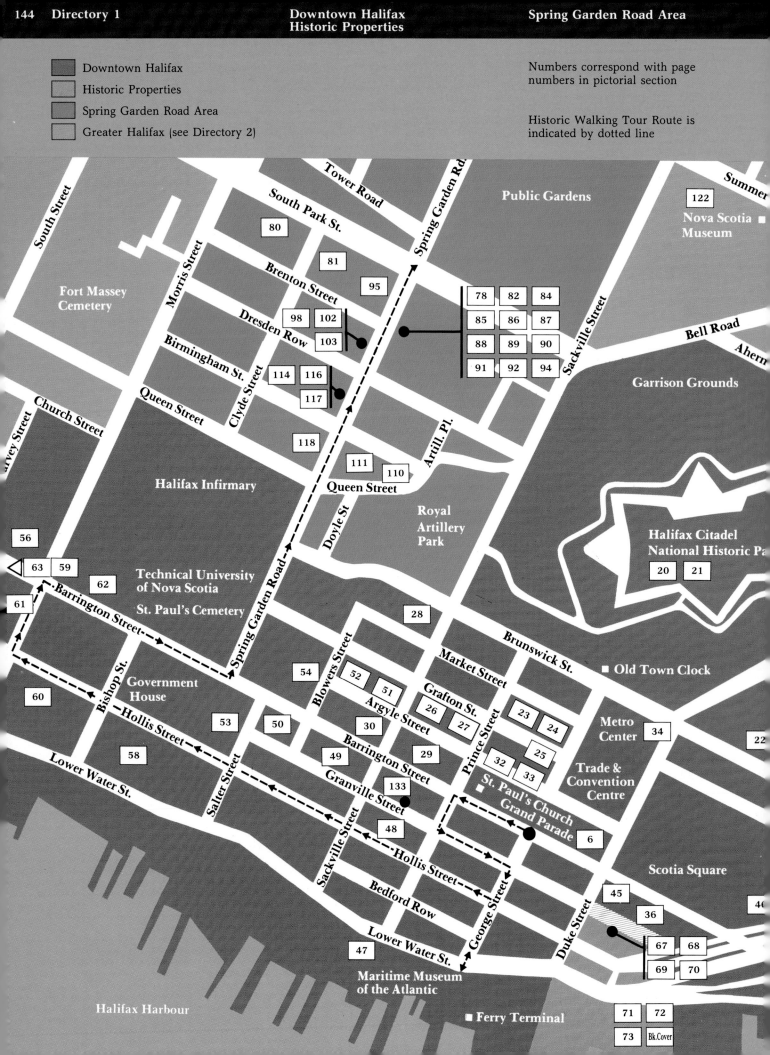

Downtown Halifax

Historic Properties

Spring Garden Road Area

Greater Halifax (see Directory 2)

Numbers correspond with page numbers in pictorial section

Historic Walking Tour Route is indicated by dotted line

Tea with the Mayor 6
Halifax Hall,
City Hall,
1841 Argyle Street,
Halifax, Nova Scotia B3J 3A5
(902) 421-6448
Every weekday from 3:30 to 4:30 p.m., visitors are welcomed to "Tea with the Mayor" in Halifax Hall, City Hall. Our century-old City Hall is located in the Grand Parade, a picture-perfect setting to experience our heritage and hospitality. Group reservations to be arranged through Tourism Halifax.

Friends of the Citadel 20
P.O. Box 3116 South,
Halifax, Nova Scotia B3J 3G6
(902) 425-3923
This unusual shop is in The Cavalier Building at the Halifax Citadel National Park. It sells jewellery, books, toys, Victorian Christmas decorations and more, all reflecting the Citadel's history. Proceeds go to supporting the special events and activities of the Friends. Open March to December.

Halifax Citadel 21
National Historic Park
P.O. Box 1480 North Postal Station,
Halifax, Nova Scotia B3K 5H7
(902) 426-5080
The Halifax Citadel is situated on a hill overlooking the heart of downtown Halifax. It was constructed between 1828 and 1856 on the site of three previous fortifications, dating to 1749. Although never attacked, the Citadel was used by the British Army until 1906 and then by the Canadian Military until after World War II.

The Citadel Halifax 22
1960 Brunswick Street,
Halifax, Nova Scotia B3J 2G7
(902) 422-1391
The Citadel Halifax has been renowned for years as one of Atlantic Canada's leading hotels. Located in downtown near historic Citadel Hill, The Citadel features 260 spacious guest rooms, an indoor pool and fitness center and complete meeting facilities. Arthur's dining room offers fine cuisine and friendly service in a delightful atmosphere.

Bistro Too Cafe-Grill-Bar 23
1770 Market Street
RCR Restaurants Ltd.
5426 Portland Place
Halifax, N.S. B3K 1A1 (902) 420-9494
A warm cheerful (but slightly sophisticated) bistro, offering traditional hearty French bistro fare with many innovative touches. Located steps from Neptune Theatre and the Metro Centre, it is ideal for dinner before the show or a delectable dessert afterwards. The best live jazz east of Montreal Thursday to Sunday evenings. Open every day.

The Prince George Hotel 24
1725 Market Street,
Halifax, Nova Scotia B3J 3N9
(902) 425-1986
The Prince George, Halifax's most elegant hotel features finely appointed guest rooms, complete recreation facilities and award winning cuisine. Crown Floor Six offers the ultimate in luxury including complimentary breakfast service. Located in the heart of downtown, the hotel is attached by underground walkway to the World Trade & Convention Center.

Cheers Lounge 25
1743 Grafton Street,
Halifax, Nova Scotia B3J 2C6
(902) 421-1655
A friendly spot with lots to offer. Lunch is served daily till 3 p.m., featuring a roast beef bar as a house specialty. Saturday brunch has a "build your own omelette bar". The portions are generous and prices are modest. Live entertainment Monday to Saturday, 10 p.m. till 2 a.m. Dance to the sounds of some of the top names in R & B and contemporary music.

Grafton Street Dinner Theatre 25
1741 Grafton Street,
Halifax, Nova Scotia B3J 2C6
(902) 425-1961
Grafton Street Dinner Theatre is the home to a unique form of entertainment that returns the audience to eras of the past. There are two musical comedies to choose from year round and the reasonable ticket price includes a hearty four course meal. Reservations required.

Alfredo, Weinstein and Ho Restaurant 25
1739 Grafton Street, Halifax, Nova Scotia B3J 2C6, (902) 421-1977
Italian, Jewish and Chinese cuisine in one restaurant! Two favourites: Ho's Combination and Bellybuster Pizza. Average cheque $8.00. Luncheon specials $3.95, brunch specials Saturday and Sunday, late night specials after 10 p.m. Relaxed, fun atmosphere, colourful, casual decor. Open Sunday 11 a.m. to 12 a.m., Monday to Thursday 11 a.m. to 3 a.m., Friday to Saturday 11 a.m. to 4 a.m. Group bookings up to 80.

Cindy's Bar.B.Q. & Fishery 26
1599 Grafton Street, P.O. Box 1013
Armdale, Nova Scotia B3L 4K9
(902) 422-8524
Set in one of the most distinguishing buildings in old Halifax, Cindy's Bar.B.Q. and Fishery reflects Louisiana Acadian roots with beautiful wrought iron and stucco, reminiscent of New Orleans and a menu featuring Cajun specialties and Nova Scotia seafood. Cindy's Bar.B.Q. occupies one half of the structure next to Halifax's most established Italian restaurant, Papa Gino's Cookery.

Unicorn Trading Company Limited 27
1579 Grafton Street,
Halifax, Nova Scotia B3J 2C3
(902) 423-4308
On entering the Unicorn, it's hard to believe that it was once a fire hall. This stunning, unique fashion store offers a wide range of top quality designer clothes for both men and women and, in the Victorian room, a wonderful assortment of accessories for the home may be found.

Cambridge Suites 28
1583 Brunswick Street,
Halifax, Nova Scotia B3J 3P5
(902) 420-0555
Cambridge Suites features 200 mini and one bedroom suites, each with separate living and sleeping areas and equipped with microwave, fridge and dishes. Complimentary breakfast is served daily and complimentary grocery shopping service is available. A fitness centre includes whirlpool, sauna and exercise equipment. Located in downtown Halifax just off Spring Garden Road.

Pino's 29
1663 Argyle Street,
Halifax, Nova Scotia B3J 2B5
(902) 420-1882
Pino's melds an extensive Italian menu with an impressive international wine list. Our restaurants are small, providing an informal, cozy atmosphere, in which to sample our Pizza, Pasta or any of our loftier meals. We celebrate our sixth year with the addition of our second location in Halifax.

Neptune Theatre 30
Corner of Sackville and Argyle Streets
Halifax, Nova Scotia B3J 2B2
(902) 429-7300
Professional theatre of the highest quality is presented each year between October and May. Neptune is situated in the heart of the city and has seen most of the stars of Canadian theatre on its stage during its 25-year history. The theatre foundation also has a young company, a theatre school and a second stage.

Lawrence of Oregano 32
1726 Argyle Street,
Halifax, Nova Scotia B3J 2B6
(902) 422-7660
This popular downtown pub offers dancing, live entertainment and affordable Italian cuisine. Built within the original Clark Company Auctioneer House (constructed in 1840), Larry O's has since expanded into three distinct sections, each with its own unique atmosphere. Established in 1980, Lawrence's is part of Halifax tradition.

My Apartment   32
1740 Argyle Street,
Halifax, Nova Scotia B3J 2B6
(902) 422-5453
Halifax's most popular nightspot. Lunch is served Monday to Friday from 11:30 a.m. to 2:30 p.m. On Saturday, one of the city's best brunches is served from 11 a.m. to 3 p.m. The nighttime offers lots of action featuring live bands, DJ music, light show and dancing. A must to visit when in the city. Open 11 a.m. to 2 a.m. Mon. to Sat. All major credit cards accepted.

The Five Fishermen Restaurant   33
1740 Argyle Street, Halifax, Nova Scotia B3J 2B6, (902) 422-4421
Enjoy conversation and friendly atmosphere within the stone and timber walls of this 1816 establishment. The finest of Maritime cuisine skillfully prepared to delight the most discriminating tastes. Tease your palate with fresh salmon, trout, halibut and Atlantic lobster. We boast Halifax's largest fresh 'catch of the day'. Entrees include complimentary salad and mussel bar. Open daily at 5 p.m. Reservations recommended.

Nova Scotia International Tattoo   34
Halifax Metro Centre,
P.O. Box 3233 South,
Halifax, Nova Scotia B3J 3H5
(902) 420-1114
Canada's largest annual indoor show with a cast of over 1800. A spectacular production of music, action and colour, that features military bands from around the world as well as civilian dancers, gymnasts and a large choir. Top international and Canadian performers will provide variety, fun, and excitement for the family. Annually in late June — early July.

The Delta Barrington   36
1875 Barrington Street,
Halifax, Nova Scotia B3J 3L6
(902) 429-7410
The Delta Barrington is seen as Halifax's country inn at the heart of the city. Its 210 guestrooms are uniquely decorated to make you feel at home. A full service, first class hotel, we offer guests superb dining, a great lounge and a full recreational centre. Inquire about our children's specials.

Daskalides' Authentic Belgian Chocolates   38
Barrington Place,
1903 Barrington Street,
Halifax, Nova Scotia B3J 3L7
(902) 422-4501
Exquisite pralines, chocolates, liqueurs, chocolate roses, cookies and fancy molded chocolates imported from famous Dask in Ghent, Belgium. Winners of The Laurier d'Or. Waffle cones hand made in store complement our delicious ice cream.

Barrington Place   38
Corner Duke, Granville
& Barrington Streets,
P.O. Box 966, Scotia Square, Halifax,
Nova Scotia B3J 2V9, (902) 429-3660
Behind a 19th century facade lies a contemporary shopping experience. Boutiques are a favourite of those in search of high quality clothing, footwear and unique merchandise. Visitors will appreciate the selection of souvenirs and take-home gifts, as well as the variety of dining possibilities, including steak bars, a Greek cafe and a lively pub.

The Paper Garden/Columbine   40
Barrington Place
Halifax, Nova Scotia B3J 3L7
(902) 423-3182
The Paper Garden is a charming shop specializing in beautiful and unusual stationery, cards and wrap. Many interesting gifts are featured, including Filofax organizers and Montblanc writing instruments. Also located in Barrington Place is Columbine, offering a range of toiletries and special foods, including, Crabtree and Evelyn.

The Doll House   41
Barrington Place,
Halifax, Nova Scotia B3J 3L7
(902) 425-5798
The Doll House, located in Barrington Place, is full of unique toys and gifts for all ages. Games, puzzles, craft and science kits, dolls and soft toys of all kinds are to be found. There are doll houses and miniatures too, from around the world.

Colwell Brothers Inc.   42
Barrington Place, P.O. Box 275,
Halifax, Nova Scotia B3J 2N7
(902) 420-1222
Colwell's offers shoppers an incomparable selection of merchandise featuring top names in fashion including Aquascutum, Burberry, Susan Bristol, Woolrich, Evan Picone, Nautica, Braemar, Bugatti, J.P. Nygard and Saville Row. A superior selection, personalized service and gorgeous surroundings is guaranteed in every store. Mic Mac Mall, Dartmouth; Barrington Place, Halifax; Brunswick Square, Saint John.

MacDonald Tobacco and Gifts   43
Barrington Place, 1903 Barrington Street,
Halifax, Nova Scotia B3J 3L7
(902) 423-6647
A specialty tobacco and nautical giftware store. If you are looking for that good Cuban cigar, unique pipe or tobacco, it's here, along with a huge selection of brass clocks, barometers and nautical items that would suit any sailor's fancy. There's also an abundance of decorative brass items, from hooks to doorknockers and bells to bookends. The shop also features locally made handcrafts and souvenirs.

The Plaid Place   44
Barrington Place,
1903 Barrington Street,
Halifax, Nova Scotia B3J 3L7
(902) 429-6872
You don't have to be Scottish to appreciate the many beautiful things at The Plaid Place. We can show 450 versions of the tartans. You can be measured for a kilt. Most accessories are in stock. We have beautiful sweaters, skirts and gift items including jewellery, music, pottery and much more.

A Step Up Distinctive Gifts   45
Barrington Place,
1903 Barrington Street
Halifax, Nova Scotia B3J 3L7
(902) 425-5964
A wide selection of gifts of every kind. China, Crystal, Music Boxes, Collectibles and more. Complimentary gift wrapping. Executive Gifts and Registered National Bridal Service. When you are thinking of something special, come see us — we have the solution.

Chateau Halifax   46
1990 Barrington Street,
Halifax, Nova Scotia B3J 1P2
(902) 425-6700
Located in the Scotia Square complex with its specialty shops and services, a ten-minute walk from the harbour, close to golf and fishing, and a 45 minute drive from the seafaring charm of Peggy's Cove, is the quiet luxury of Chateau Halifax, a haven of comfort and style.

Maritime Museum of the Atlantic   47
Director: David Flemming
1675 Lower Water Street, Halifax,
Nova Scotia B3J 1S3, (902) 429-8210
Focussing on the region's maritime history, the museum has a modern open exhibit and display centre and a restored 19th century ship chandler's shop. You'll find ship figureheads, tools of the shipbuilding trades, an extensive collection of ship models and naval artifacts. C.S.S. Acadia, a national historic site, is permanently tied up at one wharf. There are many special events throughout the year.

The Book Room   48
1664 Granville Street, P.O. Box 272,
Halifax, Nova Scotia B3J 2N7
(902) 423-2051
Founded in 1839, The Book Room is the oldest bookstore in Canada. We carry the largest selection of books in Eastern Canada, on almost any subject. Hardcovers, paperbacks and children's books fill the shelves and make browsing a pleasure. The selection of Nova Scotia books delights readers of all ages. We have a 'Special Order' dept. for that hard-to-find copy. Open daily incl. Sat. 9 a.m. - 5 p.m.

Fire Works Gallery   49
1569 Barrington Street,
Halifax, Nova Scotia B3J 1Z7
(902) 420-1735 or 1736
Fire Works Gallery, a fine crafts gallery specializing in objects made by the fire process ... jewellery, ceramics and glass. Featuring unique works by Canada's top artisans. A team of in-house goldsmiths at the gallery designs and creates custom jewellery by commission and displays works for sale made on the premises.

Celtic Traditions   50
1533 Barrington Street, Halifax,
Nova Scotia B3J 1Z4, (902) 420-0523
Scottish and Irish music, books and posters, Welsh tapestry, Aran knits, tartan items, lace, linens and woollens. Intricate designs in Sterling silver jewellery and china reproductions from centuries of craftmanship in the Celtic Countries of Scotland, Ireland, Wales, Isle-of-Man, Cornwall and Brittany. Shortbread, oatcakes, jams, teas and fragrance products to enjoy for yourself or as thoughtful gifts.

Duke of Argyle Gallery   51
1572 Argyle Street,
Halifax, Nova Scotia B3J 2B3
(902) 422-6669
The Duke of Argyle Gallery is located in the heart of Old Halifax. We have an outstanding collection of Atlantic Canadian Art from more than 30 artists. Within walking distance of the waterfront and historic Citadel Hill. The Gallery carries a fine selection of watercolors, oils, etchings and serigraphs.

Harbour Swan Giftware   52
1570 Argyle Street,
Halifax, Nova Scotia B3J 2B3
(902) 420-9399
Harbour Swan invites you to browse through an extensive selection of unique gifts: finely crafted pottery, decoys, wreaths, lamps, glass, Victorian accents, baskets, toiletries and designer wear. There's undoubtedly something here for everyone. A short stroll from all major hotels. Open Monday to Wednesday and Saturday 10 a.m. to 6 p.m. Thursday and Friday to 9 p.m.

Flamingo Cafe and Lounge   53
Maritime Centre,
1505 Barrington Street, Halifax,
Nova Scotia B3J 3K5, (902) 420-1051
Internationally renowned live music featuring reggae, blues, zydeco, folk, calypso and other world-roots music. The Flamingo was voted Entertainment Venue of the Year, 1989 Maritime Music Awards! Artists featured to date include John Hiatt, Billy Bragg, Burning Spear, Jane Siberry, Richard Thompson, Cowboy Junkies, Sarah MacLachlan and Buckwheat Zydeco. Food service 5 p.m. to 10 p.m.

La Cave Restaurant   54
5244 Blowers Street,
Halifax, Nova Scotia B3J 1J7
(902) 429-3551
La Cave is a cozy grotto just a step below street level. It mixes good food, such as pepper steak, chicken kiev and cheese fondue, as well as burgers and finger foods, with good music. Fully licensed. Open Tuesday and Wednesday 5 p.m. to 2 a.m., Thursday to Saturday to 4:30 a.m., and Sunday to midnight.

Waverley Inn   56
1266 Barrington Street,
Halifax, Nova Scotia B3J 1Y5
(902) 423-9346
Discover the 19th century elegance at Victorian rates! of the downtown inn within walking distance of what you want to see and do. The Waverley Mansion is tastefully furnished with antiques and period reproductions. All rooms with private bath, phone, color T.V. Enjoy complimentary breakfast, afternoon tea or late evening snacks in the Waverley breakfast room. Year round. Visa, M/C.

da Maurizio   58
The Brewery,
1496 Lower Water Street, Halifax,
Nova Scotia B3J 1R7, (902) 423-0859
Located in the Brewery, da Maurizio offers the city's finest Northern Italian cuisine. This beautiful dining room, including hand-painted walls, overlooks the harbour. Select from an extensive menu, prepared by one of Halifax's most well-known chefs, Maurizio Bertossi. Dinner selections include seafood, beef, veal, chicken and creative home-made pasta dishes. Reservations suggested. Buon appetito!

Heritage House Inn   59
1253 Barrington Street, Halifax,
Nova Scotia B3J 1Y2, (902) 423-4435
Your home away from home. An historic house decorated in period furnishings, within walking distance of all amenities. Full breakfast Monday to Friday. Continental breakfast Saturday, Sunday and Holidays. Elegant tea room open for afternoon tea. Single $36-40; Doubles & Twins $50-58; Extra person $10. Limited parking. No pets. CBTV and radio in lounge area. Pay telephone. Major credit cards.

Mary Jane's Alternative Tastes Ltd.   60
1313 Hollis Street,
Halifax, Nova Scotia B3J 1T8
(902) 421-1313
This most unusual foodstore is sure to intrigue all lovers of food. Natural and organic foods, combined with gourmet and ethnic groceries, including Mexican, Japanese and Indian, and Halifax's best selection of imported cheeses, coffees, spices, fresh breads and produce, create a unique shopping experience. Open every day. Free parking.

The Halliburton House Inn   61
5184 Morris Street,
Halifax, Nova Scotia B3J 1B3
(902) 420-0658
"This small and extremely choice hotel is now the place to stay in Halifax." Where to Eat in Canada, 1989. Fine evening dining, by reservation. Private luncheons, banquets and parties. An ideal environment for small meetings and conferences. The elegance and warmth of a traditional Inn in the heart of the city.

The Granite Brewery   62
1222 Barrington Street,
P.O. Box 114,
Halifax, Nova Scotia B3J 2L4
(902) 422-4954 & 423-5660
The Granite Brewery, located in Historic Henry House, is Eastern Canada's first Brew Pub. Two fine English style ales are brewed on the premises. The Granite Brewery is open Monday to Friday from 11:30 a.m. to 12:30 a.m., with English style pub food offered until 10:00 p.m. Brunch is served on Saturday until 4 p.m.

Halifax Hilton   63
1181 Hollis Street,
Halifax, Nova Scotia B3H 2P6
(902) 423-7231
Located on the waterfront, overlooking the Harbour and Cornwallis Park and connected to the VIA Rail Station. Recently restored, The Nova Scotian offers deluxe guestrooms with air conditioning, remote control television, in room movies, room service, a tennis court, indoor pool, sauna and whirlpool. Also the Chart Room restaurant, Pier 21 Lounge and South Street Pub.

J.J. Rossy's Bar & Grill Ltd.   67
Shooter's Dining Room and Lounge
Granville Mall,
P.O. Box 2123 Stn. "M", Halifax,
Nova Scotia B3J 3B7, (902) 422-4411
This three storey bar, in an historic building, offers a varied menu of gourmet burgers, steaks, chicken, ribs, pasta and Chinese dishes. Sat. brunch is served. Domestic and imported beers served throughout, including draught beer in the bar and spirits in the lounge. D.J. music nightly for listening and dancing. Open from 11 a.m. to 12 a.m. and 2 a.m. respectively.

The Stornoway   68
1873 Granville Street,
Halifax, Nova Scotia B3J 1Y1
(902) 422-9507
Our shop offers you the finest creations by leading Nova Scotia and Maritime artisans. Home accessories including Madawaska placemats and napkins, Cheticamp hookings, woven bedspreads from Wales. Ladies jackets and men's sweaters made in the Yukon. Many more too numerous to mention. Come let us make your stay in Halifax complete.

Christmas by the Sea   68
1880 Hollis Street,
Halifax, Nova Scotia B3J 1W6
(902) 429-6090
Christmas by the Sea is Atlantic Canada's largest year-round Christmas shop. Unique decorations from around the world adorn the many themed trees in this shop. Precious moments, treasured memories, collectibles and metro's largest selection of music boxes are part of their unique lines. Bring your camera when you visit.

The Sweater Shop   69
1870 Hollis Street,
Halifax, Nova Scotia B3J 1W5
(902) 422-9209
"An outlet store at its best". This was our first mill outlet store and it's still the best. The finest of wools handframed to a variety of styles to suit anyone's lifestyle. Natural oil, plain and super wash wools. P.S. We also make cottons and sell great accessories.

The Pewter House   70
Granville Mall, 1875 Granville Street,
Halifax, Nova Scotia B3J 1Y1
(902) 423-8843
For the Atlantic provinces' finest offering of local and imported pewter, giftware, jewellery, tableware and much more, be sure to visit The Pewter House, where you'll see its unique gift ideas displayed on a collection of period furniture. An ideal place to find that perfect gift. Open Monday to Wednesday and Saturday 9:30 a.m. to 5:30 p.m. Thursday and Friday to 9 p.m.

The James House of Fine China   71
Historic Properties,
1869 Upper Water Street,
Halifax, Nova Scotia B3J 1S9
(902) 429-2355
Located in Historic Properties, The James House offers you the largest selection of Waterford crystal and Wedgwood china in the Maritimes, along with Stuart crystal, Belleek and Portmeirion. Visit our figurine room for Coalport, Hummel and Lladro figurines. Open all year round.

Halifax Water Tours   72
Historic Properties,
1869 Upper Water Street,
Halifax, Nova Scotia B3J 1S9
(902) 423-1271
Nova Scotia's most popular two-hour watertour with complete commentary. Depart from Historic Properties, tour historic Halifax Harbour and the beautiful Northwest Arm, a haven of elegant residences and sail craft. Our tour will show you an exciting contrast between Halifax's historic past with its modern influences. All aboard The Haligonian III!

Clipper Cay   73
Historic Properties,
Host Restaurateurs Limited,
P.O. Box 3605 South, Halifax,
Nova Scotia B3J 3K6, (902) 423-6818
Halifax's Window on the Waterfront. Nestled in the heart of famous Historic Properties, the Clipper Cay gives diners a front row view of Halifax Harbour — one of the busiest ports in the world — through floor to ceiling windows. Award-winning chefs create succulent dishes from steaming seafood platters to fresh pastas and decadent desserts.

Historic Feast Company   Back Cover
The Banquet Hall, Simon's Warehouse,
Historic Properties,
Halifax, Nova Scotia B3J 1S9
(902) 420-1840
Step into the Feast for dinner theatre right out of 1840's Halifax. Talented musicians and actors serve up a sumptuous four-course meal and light-hearted frivolity as they lure the audience into antics. The Historic Feast Company — an entertaining indulgence.

Spring Garden Road Area   78
Business Improvement District Commission
Suite 104, 5435 Spring Garden Road,
Halifax, N.S. B3J 1G1, (902) 423-3751
The Commission represents over 335 businesses and services in an area situated south of the Citadel and nearby historic Public Gardens. This area is close to most major hotels. Atlantic Canada's best shopping and dining can be experienced and, with over 200 specialty shops and 2,000 parking spaces, a trip to this area will be exciting, easy and fun.

Le Bistro Cafe   80
1333 South Park Street,
RCR Restaurants, 5426 Portland Place,
Halifax, Nova Scotia B3K 1A1
(902) 423-8428
A sunny garden atrium humming with conversation and spiced with the aroma of good strong coffee ..... a little bit of France in Halifax? Oui. With a tantalizing main course menu and a mouth-watering array of superb desserts, it's no wonder that the Bistro Cafe remains Halifax's most popular bistro. Open every day.

Sanford's Dining Room and Wine Cellar Cafe   81
5677 Brenton Place, Halifax,
Nova Scotia B3J 1E4, (902) 422-1466
Sanford's enjoys a reputation for good food and pleasant service. With an extensive menu of seafood, meats and pasta, there's something for everyone. The more casual Wine Cellar Cafe offers lighter snacks, wine by the glass and an excellent choice of imported beers. Sanford's is the place for lunch, dinner or just a snack. Two outdoor seating areas in summer. Non Smoking floor. Major credit cards.

Shops at Park Lane   82
Park Lane Developments Ltd.
5657 Spring Garden Road,
Halifax, Nova Scotia B3J 3R4
(902) 420-9799
Park Lane has gathered together a fine collection of over 60 shops — international and casual fashions, gifts, jewellery, cards, books, flowers and more. There's a cozy cafe, your favourite eateries, eight superbly comfortable cinemas and parking. Park Lane — in the heart of Halifax. Mon. Tues & Sat. 9:30 a.m. - 6 p.m. Weds. Thurs. Fri. 9:30 a.m. - 9:30 p.m.

The Food Court   82
Park Lane
5657 Spring Garden Road,
Halifax, Nova Scotia B3J 3R4
The Food Court offers an array of international foods! Try the Mexican, Hungarian or Chinese cuisine, hamburgers, salads, freshly-made sandwiches or traditional fish and chips. Finish off with a delicious frozen yogurt treat or savour the delights from the bake shop — gourmet cookies, giant muffins and much more.

The Greenery Florists   82
Park Lane,
5657 Spring Garden Road,
Halifax, Nova Scotia B3J 3R4
(902) 423-7496
The Greenery Florists are a locally owned chain of full-service flower shops that offer high quality silks and giftware. Our fresh-cut flowers range from traditional to the exotic with our floral designers always available to assist you in making the perfect choice for your home, that special gift or occasion.

Rodier Femmes/Rodier Hommes   84
Park Lane, 5657 Spring Garden Road,
Halifax, Nova Scotia B3J 3R4
(902) 422-6595
A unique, side-by-side concept in Ladies' and Men's French fashion in an elegant, quiet atmosphere. Knowledgeable staff will guide you through this European fashion experience with a smile. Rodier's reputation for great style and top quality is responsible for worldwide success in the fashion industry. Located in Park Lane, the most beautiful shopping complex in the Maritimes.

Club Monaco   85
Park Lane, 5657 Spring Garden Road,
Halifax, N.S. B3J 3R4, (902) 425-2878
Club Monaco began as a concept: an entertaining, compelling environment purveying the ultimate basic, casual quality wear for men, women, and kids. Club Monaco achieves a keynote of "sustained classicism" in its approach to basic style and natural fibres. This neighborhood emporia of lifestyle products encompasses everything from clothing and accessories, to fragrance and unique items for personal or home use. Welcome to the Club!

John David Shoes Ltd   86
Park Lane, 5657 Spring Garden Road,
Halifax, Nova Scotia B3J 3R4
(902) 422-8466
Located in the heart of downtown shopping is Halifax's newest addition to footwear fashion, catering to both men and women. Sperry, Rockport, 9-West and Jasmin are just a few of the names you'll find at John David Shoes. Come in and see the professionally trained sales team at John David and experience quality footwear at affordable prices.

Heritage Pewter   87
Park Lane, 5657 Spring Garden Road,
P.O. Box 120, Halifax,
Nova Scotia B3J 3R4, (902) 422-7667
We invite you to experience the old-world charm and contemporary styling of pewter. Creations by maritime pewtersmiths and imports from international artisans assure a pleasing selection — both unique and whimsical. Accessorize with our beautiful Portmeirion tableware in "Botanic Garden" pattern, designed by Susan Williams-Ellis of Great Britain.

Madame Angelo   88
Park Lane, 5657 Spring Garden Road,
P.O. Box 153,
Halifax, Nova Scotia B3J 3R4
(902) 423-9864
Each accessory from Madame Angelo has its own raison d'etre, its own integrity of design. Each has its own originality of concept making it timeless in its perfection. From exquisite sweaters to the special élan of a broad-brimmed hat. From the glitter of a sparkling earring to the delicacy of a well stitched glove. Accessories to cherish. Accessories to charm.

Jewellery by Fusion Design   89
Park Lane,
5657 Spring Garden Road,
Box 200,
Halifax, Nova Scotia B3J 3R4
(902) 423-0775
At Fusion Design, we feature unique jewellery by local designers. This is complimented by a selection of contemporary crafts, including glass, clocks, sculpture and more. Also, visit our Halifax Shopping Centre location for a slightly different look at Nova Scotia crafts.

La Maison Bleue Distinctive   90
Handcrafts
Park Lane, Box 170,
5657 Spring Garden Road, Halifax,
Nova Scotia B3J 3R4 (902) 423-2555
Located within Park Lane on Spring Garden Road, you will discover some of the finest and most unique handcrafts in Nova Scotia. From Porcelain figurines, pottery, paintings, quilts, rugs, jewellery, wood sculptures to one-of-a-kind clothing designs. Discover this and much more. Mon. Tues. Sat. 9:30 a.m. - 6 p.m.; Wed. Thurs. Fri. 9:30 a.m. - 9:30 p.m.

JJ. Farmer   91
Park Lane,
5657 Spring Garden Road,
Halifax, Nova Scotia B3J 3R4
(902) 422-2992
At JJ. Farmer, we offer a collection of casual and comfortable clothing, complemented by a unique selection of handcrafted items. In keeping with the country look of our fashions is an impressive array of items that combine art with craft. The spirit of JJ. Farmer is rooted in tradition. If you share our vision and values, you will feel at home in JJ. Farmer country.

Rodney's   92
Spring Garden Road, Halifax,
Nova Scotia B3J 3R4, (902) 423-8807
Rodney's, formerly House of Rodney in the Lord Nelson Arcade, continues its tradition of high quality fashion leadership in its new Park Lane location. The new Rodney's store offers the highest of contemporary merchandising standards while retaining the warmth and charm of the previous location of 27 years. Rodney's ranks among the finest men's wear stores in Canada. Invest in your appearance with a visit to Rodney's in Park Lane.

Rapport   92
Park Lane
5657 Spring Garden Road
Halifax, Nova Scotia B3J 3R4
(902) 422-6137
Discover Rapport, a small friendly shop where women are finding clothing with the style, fit and quality they've been looking for. Contemporary classics by Jacques Vert, for career or weekend wear, are offered in sizes 4 to 16. Alain Cannelle, a new line of active sportswear by Jacques Vert, rounds out this lifestyle collection.

The Body Shop   94
Park Lane,
5657 Spring Garden Road,
Halifax, Nova Scotia B3J 3R4
(902) 423-6671
We produce products that cleanse, polish and protect the skin and hair. We are innovative in our formulations; we are passionate about environmental and social issues; we care about retailing. The image, goals and values of our company are as important as our products. Our Mission Statement! We will be the most honest cosmetics company around.

Pepe's Dining Room and Lounge   95
5680 Spring Garden Road,
Halifax, Nova Scotia B3J 1H5
(902) 429-7321
Light lunches, full course dinners or late night cravings. Specializing in seafood, steaks and roast beef, with a bakery on the premises. A small cozy conversation bar and two working fireplaces. Casual or formal, you will feel comfortable.

Spring Garden Place   98
Spring Garden Services Ltd.
5640 Spring Garden Road,
P.O. Box 3490 South,
Halifax, Nova Scotia B3J 2J2
(902) 429-3060
Spring Garden Place is a cozy six-level mall featuring 32 specialty shops and unique food market on the lower level. Among the boutiques are children's shops, fashions, leather goods, an award-winning jewellery shop, a flower shop . . . Open Mon. to Wed. and Sat. 9 a.m. - 5:30 p.m.; Thurs. and Fri. to 9 p.m.

Le Femme Lingerie   98
Spring Garden Place,
5640 Spring Garden Road, Halifax,
Nova Scotia, B3J 3M7, (902) 423-5888
La Femme features a wide range of lingerie, from the lacier French imports to the more conventional styles — nightgowns, bath robes, peignoir sets, slips, bras, panties, stockings and swimwear are just some of the items to be found. We offer personalized service and love to cater to the man looking for that special gift. Free gift wrapping offered. Also on lower level of Scotia Square. (420-9045)

Lifestyle Fashions   99
Spring Garden Place
5640 Spring Garden Road,
Halifax, Nova Scotia B3J 3M7
(902) 423-2800
Lifestyle Fashions features separates and accessories for the fashion-conscious woman, who likes to create her own look. Here the customer can find mixables from well-known brands such as Mexx and Jump and also one-of-a kind pieces selected just for the store. Lifesyle's aim is to make good quality fashion both fun and affordable for women of all ages.

Bratz Children's Wear   100
Spring Garden Place,
5640 Spring Garden Road
Halifax, Nova Scotia, B3J 3M7
(902) 423-5857
Where you'll find the largest selection of quality fashions for youth, from such great names as Esprit, Mexx, Levi, Non-Fiction, Polo by Ralph Lauren and more. Friendly staff and complete refund policy make shopping at Halifax's trendiest spot for sizes 2-20 a must.

Rye 'N' Pickle   100
Spring Garden Place
5640 Spring Garden Road,
Halifax, Nova Scotia B3J 3M7
(902) 423-6664 & 422-4222
Nestled in the Market at Spring Garden Place is Halifax's most prestigious Delicatessen and Butcher Shop, the Rye 'N' Pickle. Noted for its world famous cheeses, Montreal smoked meats, kosher breads and the finest selection of fresh meat in Halifax, the Rye 'N' Pickle is a great combination of quality and personality plus. Open 7 days a week.

Frog Hollow Books   101
Spring Garden Place,
5640 Spring Garden Road, Halifax,
Nova Scotia, B3J 3M7, (902) 424-3318
Customers can make use of two comfortable
armchairs to browse through books before
making a selection. The store stocks a wide
variety of best sellers, both paperback and
hard cover, along with classics, mysteries,
biographies, new age and local interest books.
Frog Hollow prides itself on selecting books
which pique the imagination and stimulate the
interest of those who enjoy reading.

The Bakery & Cafe   101
Spring Garden Place
5640 Spring Garden Road,
Halifax, Nova Scotia B3J 3M7
(902) 425-6529
The Spring Garden Bakery & Cafe offers a
light breakfast menu in a relaxing atmosphere.
The menu ranges from freshly baked quiche
to delicious home-made muffins. For lunch,
home-made soups, hot entrees, fresh salads
and sandwiches await you. Don't forget to
take home a loaf of freshly baked bread.

A Touch of Gold   102
Spring Garden Place,
5640 Spring Garden Road, P.O. Box 544,
Halifax, N.S. B3J 2R7, (902) 423-5600
Touch of Gold has captured both Canadian
Jewellery Design Awards, in 1988 the Canadian Jeweller "Editor's Choice Award" and
the DeBeer's "Diamonds Today" in 1989.
Focus is on custom design, loose and mounted
gems, high-fashion gold and silver jewellery.
Professional jewellery services include re-
modelling, repair and appraisal. Exclusive
agents for "Cartier" and "Rolex" watches.

Ryan Duffy's Steak & Seafood   103
Spring Garden Place,
5640 Spring Garden Road,
RCR Restaurants, 5426 Portland Place,
Halifax, Nova Scotia B3K 1A1
(902) 421-1116
Your waiter will cut and trim your steak right
at your table to your requirements before grill-
ing it to perfection over natural wood char-
coal. Seafood lover? The "fresh sheet" lists
only the fish the chef received fresh that day.
Drop into Duffy's Bar for a relaxing drink
before or after your meal. Open every day.

The Pepper Pot   110
1549 Birmingham Street (at Queen),
Halifax, N.S. B3J 2J6, (902) 425-4146
More than just a kitchen store, it's a warm,
multi-leveled boutique; a shopper's paradise
of household gifts and furnishings. Unique
lines carry up-to-date looks, hand-blown
Mexican glassware, vibrant dinnerware from
the Gulf of Naples and signed Brazilian pottery. The Pepper Pot — looks that contribute
to good quality interiors. Monday to Saturday
9:30 a.m. to 5:30 p.m. Thursday and Friday
till 9:30 p.m.

Cricklewood Giftware Inc.   111
1529 Birmingham Street,
Halifax, Nova Scotia B3J 2J6
(902) 423-1604
"Gifts of love for hearts of all ages" describes
the variety of giftwares and crafts located in
a century old home. Featuring international
lines, beautiful handcrafts, one-of-a-kind finds
and unique objects in a blend of Victoriana
and country. Superb service and friendly
charm make this shop unique.

Natal Day Festival   112
P.O. Box 1749
Halifax, Nova Scotia B3J 3A5
(902) 421-6448
On the first Monday in August, Halifax cele-
brates its birthday. The Natal Day Festival is
a weekend birthday party complete with a
parade, concerts and spectacular fireworks.
Everyone is invited to the Capital City for the
exciting celebration.

Maritime Frame-It   114
5512 Spring Garden Road,
National Art Limited,
5426 Portland Place, Halifax,
Nova Scotia B3K 1A1, (902) 423-7117
While visiting Halifax, don't miss one of the
city's most unique shops, Maritime Frame-It.
Browse amongst our huge selection of framed
and unframed art, world-renowned W.R.
MacAskill (1890-1956) hand-coloured photographs, unique gifts and much, much more.
Maritime Frame-It has five easy-to-find loca-
tions in Halifax and Dartmouth to serve you.

The Tweed Shop   116
5516 Spring Garden Road,
Halifax, Nova Scotia B3J 1G6
(902) 423-8755
Where everyone receives friendly, personal
attention. A European flavour is evident in the
merchandise as well as in the expertise of the
sales staff. The very best of ladies' fashions
from France, Britain, Austria, Ireland, Holland
and Canada have been carefully selected for
you. Feel free to browse.

Winsbys Limited   117
5504 Spring Garden Rod,
Halifax, Nova Scotia B3J 1G5
(902) 423-7324
One of Canada's finest women's shoe stores
is a must for shoppers visiting Halifax.
Winsbys is located in the heart of Halifax's
quality street — Spring Garden Road. A large
selection of brand names, styles, sizes and
widths, combined with personalized service,
explains why Winsbys has such a loyal
following.

Mills Brothers Ltd.   118
5486 Spring Garden Road,
P.O. Box 9198 Station A,
Halifax, Nova Scotia B3K 5M8
(902) 429-6111
Established in 1919. A unique shopping experience and landmark on the "most walked"
street in Halifax. Twelve special shops on two
floors include fine fashions, perfumes and
cosmetics for women and men, as well as
lingerie, accessories and a Crabtree and
Evelyn Shop. Open Mon. to Sat. 9 a.m. to 5:30
p.m. Thurs. & Fr. 9 a.m. to 9 p.m.